77
ic

2. 2.

The Game
with the Hole in it

The Game
with the Hole in it

*

PETER DOBEREINER

FABER AND FABER

London

First published in 1970
by Faber and Faber Limited
24 Russell Square London WC1
Reprinted 1970
Printed in Great Britain by
Latimer Trend & Co Ltd Plymouth
All rights reserved

ISBN 0 571 08923 2

Dedicated to my other favourite sport

My wife, B.E.D.

Contents

Introduction		*page*	9
1.	A bastard of a game		13
2.	Our mother, that sad old bitch		29
3.	March of the gladiators		46
4.	Golf is people		65
5.	Golf clubs and how not to throw them		84
6.	Trembling on the lip		101
7.	Woman's place is in the what?		117
8.	You're supposed to enjoy it		127

ILLUSTRATIONS

The plates between pages 88 and 89
illustrate the swing of the club

Photographs by Chris Smith,
by courtesy of the *Observer*

Introduction

THEY say that converts are more rabid than those born into a faith. My own case, in regard to golf, certainly bears out that theory. For although I was exposed to the game early—my first paid employment was to pick up stones scuffed on to the turf from the gravel paths of a putting course in New York in the late 1920's—I escaped infection. I was then four years old and remember that at the end of the first week I was paid a dime. Within half an hour I had blued the lot on a penknife, cut my hand and had the knife confiscated by my mother.

That experience may partly explain my opinion of putting as an exasperating and futile activity. It is an important part of the game, of course, rather too important in my view, but unworthy of being dignified by strong emotions or intense application. 'Miss 'em quick' is an old and sound adage.

The childhood experience may also have been responsible for souring my attitude to work. I have never been able to recognise much logic, except in theoretical terms and in relation to other people at that, in the concept of hard work being virtuous of itself. After many years in many jobs I have at last achieved a satisfactory compromise between my natural lethargy and the need to eat. My work is my play; my play is my work. Golf has allowed me to indulge this selfish philosophy. My life consists mainly of playing it badly, watching it being played well, and writing about it for *The Observer*.

Envious people often ask: 'How do you become a golf correspondent?' There is no approved method; all the golf writers I know drifted into the job by accident. In my case the apprenticeship started in the late 1940's when I was working in India for a large company which refined sugar and distilled whisky, gin and brandy of such vile quality that I have been virtually teetotal ever since.

For much of my stay in Travancore there were only three other European males and so I was conscripted, with mutual reluctance and misgivings, as a makeweight fourth for bridge, tennis and golf.

It happened that the English tutor of the Maharajah of Travancore had been a keen golfer and had prevailed on the royal family to build a nine-hole course to further the young prince's social education. The Maharajah didn't much care for the game and gave it up as soon as he became old enough to please himself.

But the course was beautifully maintained and, apart from rare golf-playing guests at the palace, was used at the Maharajah's kind invitation only by our fourball. Each of us had two caddies, of course, one to carry the bag and a forecaddie to run ahead and mark the position of the ball. The cost of such luxury, by the way, amounted to a total of 2s. 3d. a round, including generous tips.

The fairways of this equatorial course were sun-baked and drives bounced for flattering distances, almost as if on concrete. And, thanks to the forecaddies, shots hit off line, slicing and hooking did not matter. If one of us carved one way into the rough, his forecaddie rushed to the spot, picked up the ball between his toes and strolled nonchalantly back to the centre of the fairway depositing the errant missile on a coaxing cushion of grass. Often in my case, he leapt the boundary wall and saved his sahib the embarrassment of penalty strokes. I regret to say that our efforts to discourage this scandalous practice were not over-emphatic. Compassion proved stronger than our legalistic conscience; after all, the boys were only trying to ingratiate themselves in the hope of a good tip and we, all too aware of their poverty, became easily ingratiated. Cheating it may have been, but it was the same for everyone. Even today I cannot raise much of an incredulous whistle at the massive hitting of golfers such as David Thomas and Jack Nicklaus. For

INTRODUCTION

I cannot forget that I once drove as far as any muscular professional and with never a stray one into snake country.

For all that, or perhaps because of it, I became irrevocably touched by the spell of this great game. The love-hate affair has lasted ever since and eventually led me into the field of professional golf writing. Fanaticism is basically my only qualification.

Looked at with clinical detachment, golf is a simple and basically absurd pastime. What would Socrates have said if he had been told that one day men skilled in knocking a ball over a hill with a stick would be esteemed above philosophers and rewarded many times higher than great statesmen? Something pithy, no doubt. But golfers cannot be objective about their sport. Emotions, even passions, are involved the moment a man first takes club in hand. It looks so easy, just a matter of hitting a stationary ball. Man, a natural tool-using animal, is born to just such an implement as a golf club. He takes an atavistic swipe. And probably misses. At that moment a golfer is born. It is so patently simple and yet, in practice, so fiendishly difficult. *There* is the fascination of golf—the urge to reconcile these two evident yet contradictory truths.

Everyone knows he is physically capable of hitting a perfect shot. Occasionally he is reinforced in this belief by actually doing so. It follows that any person is theoretically capable of stringing together a series of shots to constitute a perfect round of golf. No one has done it yet and it is quite safe to predict that no one ever will.

Every week the lure of golf attracts more recruits to the course. My purpose in writing this book is to provide a brief introduction to the world of golf for newcomers who may wish to know something of the enormous ramifications of the game. Instant golf lore. My intentions are neither scholarly nor technical nor comprehensive. The book, I hope, is more like a game of golf itself—a leisurely stroll with occasional halts for business but without ever forgetting, as the great American golfer Walter Hagen insisted, to smell the flowers along the way.

An impressive case could be made out for golf as an important thread in the fabric of our society, as a force for good in an evil world, as a healthy counterpart to the stress society. But not by me. Golf is a game. It is more than 'just a game' but a game nevertheless. Its purpose is to provide pleasure. This book is my attempt to give to others something of the pleasure that golf has given to me.

I

A bastard of a game

WE need not linger over the origins of golf. Historians and scholars have argued at tedious length about the game's parentage. This eminent authority claims that the French game of *chole* fathered golf; another states with no less conviction that the Dutch *kolven* was the true progenitor. Yet another points the finger of suspicion at *jeu de mall*.

There is little doubt in my mind that they are all mistaken. Golf is a bastard.

Man, we are told, is distinguished from other living species by his capacity for speech, imagination and the use of tools. And there we have the essential requirements for golf—the ability to judge a shot, the power to execute it and the faculty for shouting 'Damn!' as the ball plummets into a thorn bush.

Anthropologists seeking the missing link need ask themselves only one question as they inspect a likely skeleton: Could this creature have played golf? If the answer is yes, they have their man; if no, it is just an ape.

The appeal of golf is elemental. Just as a newly born baby instinctively grabs his rattle, albeit with a hooker's grip, so a grown man who is presented with a club cannot resist the primitive promptings to pick it up and swipe at something.

And so golf is not a game that was suddenly invented, or even imported into Scotland from heathen lands. Clearly it evolved, slowly and naturally, as we can see from the writings of earliest times. We know, for instance, that the Normans and Saxons were 'driving balls wide over the fields' at the coronation of King

13

Arthur in 872 and, although it wasn't golf as we know it, the seed had obviously begun to sprout. The golf historian Robert Browning makes the valid point that 'the idea of hitting a ball with a crooked stick—as, for instance, in the simplest form of pall-mall, where the rivalry consists merely of seeing which player can send the ball farthest—is so primitive as to be common to all countries'.

From such fundamental beginnings, different games were refined according to national temperament and the availability of natural materials for the construction of the implements of play.

In Britain archery was an important part of life. And so it was natural, almost inevitable, that a ball and stick game should be strongly influenced by the arts and traditions of the bowmaker. It is no coincidence that the wooden shafts of the early golf clubs bore a similarity to the arrows of the long bow. They were both made by the same craftsmen. The first written references to an individual golfer are the 1502 records of payments to the bowar of St. Johnestown for clubbis and ballis for King James IV of Scotland who was known as James the Iron Belt, not a bad nickname for a golfer.

But long before then, in 1457, James II (James of the Fiery Face —and there's another appropriate golfing soubriquet) became alarmed at the way his subjects were being seduced from archery practice by more diverting pastimes and decreed that 'the futeball and golfe be utterly cryed down and not to be used'.

If Fiery Face was perturbed that golf was deflecting the Scots from the path of the national duty to knock hell out of the English, it is clear that the game was well established at the time. I like to conjecture that even in King Arthur's day some of the rudiments of golf were established.

Among these stalwarts driving balls wide over the fields there must surely have been men famous for their skill, champions who worked out the most effective techniques and passed on their skills, for a consideration, by advising pupils to 'keep ye swiving left arm straight!'

If archery explains the evolution of club making, then the topography of Scotland provides all the clues we need to see how the game itself developed. Golf courses are basically artificial copies of the natural shoreline of eastern Scotland. The linksland, stretches of grassland cropped short by sheep and pocked by small pits where scars in the turf had exposed the sand to be scooped away and scattered by the winds. The links, formed by the receding sea and unsuitable for arable cultivation, were the natural recreation spaces of the inhabitants of the fishing towns.

The women hung their washing to dry on the whin bushes of the links, the men came here for bow and arrow practice, and if you wanted to hit a ball with a stick you had to go to the links because there was nowhere else. Doubtless the nature of the linksland was a decisive factor in the making of golf. On a flat muddy meadow you would soon get bored by swatting a ball about. Given the accident of that glorious turf and those maddening depressions of sand, the business of knocking a ball along with a stick was at once pleasant and frustrating.

Every stroke presented a different challenge and the wind, constantly shifting direction and generally strong enough to cause an interesting deflection of the ball, added further to the variety.

Given a club and ball on the one hand and the Scottish linksland on the other, the outcome of the game of golf was as inevitable as the invention of an equally popular pastime when Eve was added to Adam.

The madness took firm grip of the Scots and was given impetus by royal patronage. All the Stuart kings played the game and it is to Scotland's credit that golf there has never been the exclusive preserve of one social class. Every stratum of society from fishermen to royalty enjoyed the sport and on the links at least a man's prowess with baffie and cleek was more important than his pedigree. In this respect, England was very different. Golf, when it came, was regarded a gentleman's game and remained so until well into the twentieth century. Consequently the game was slower to spread and even the much publicised enthusiasm of the Prince of Wales (later Edward VIII)—who did for golf what his grandfather had done for adultery—simply popularised golf among the Bertie Wooster belt of the flapper generation.

The democratic aspect of Scottish golf, it must be admitted, was due more to economic reasons than social enlightenment. The courses were public land and the cost of golf was therefore within the means of most people, a state of affairs which continues to this day to a degree which is the envy of golfers of every other country. Cheap golf, it is accepted, is the Scotsman's birthright.

Incidentally, if I may make a fruitless (but I hope interesting) digression into a historical cul-de-sac at this point, I have been struck by the affinity of golf and fishing. As we have seen, fishermen were largely responsible for the development of the game; the exigencies of the tide frequently found them with time on their hands during the daylight hours. And throughout the literature of the game, fish keep breaking surface. A remarkably high proportion of golfers are also devoted anglers. The life expectancy among fish would be significantly higher if there were no professional golfers. Julius Boros is famous for landing a fat bass from an ornamental pond at Augusta between rounds of the Masters; Jack Nicklaus is notorious for his preference for fish over chips; Max Faulkner can generally be found during seaside tournaments bobbing about in an open boat while his fellow competitors are abed. And there are so many more. Why do fishing and golf go together? There is the attraction of relaxing quietly with rod and line after the tensions of the course but that explanation seems altogether too glib and obvious. I cannot help feeling there is more to it than that.

Reverting to the history of golf, it is convenient to look at the game in terms of eras of development. The earliest golf balls were wooden spheres and the clubs large and clumsy implements by modern standards. Even so, they did not stand up for long to the punishment they had to take from the hard, unyielding projectiles. The introduction of the feathery ball early in the seventeenth century provided an opportunity for advances in the club-maker's art. Under the hand of craftsmen such as Hugh Philp, clubs became things of beauty and tools of increasing precision for good players.

Another Scottish club-maker, Allan Robertson, who is generally reckoned to be the first true golf professional, pioneered the manufacture of clubs with iron heads for special contingencies. Their purpose can generally be deduced from their names—driving irons and rutting irons for excavating the ball from cart tracks. One of my few regrets about advances in golf is that we have lost those marvellous names. Cleek, baffie, mashie and niblick—how much richer are these names than the impersonal numerals by which we distinguish our modern clubs.

Although it was much better than wood, the feathery ball—made from a top hat full of steamed feathers sewn into a bull-hide casing—was far from fully satisfactory. It was expensive, was ruined by a single cut, became waterlogged in wet weather and split easily at the seams.

Then in 1848 a happy accident transformed the game. A professor at St. Andrews, so the story goes, received a crate from the east containing a statuette which had been protected on its journey by a packing of gutta percha, a latex-like substance which is tapped as a resin from trees and which hardens on exposure to the air. The professor, true to thrifty Scot's tradition, was reluctant to throw away the novel, rubbery substance since he felt that there might be a useful purpose to which it could be put. Pondering the problem, and rolling a lump of gutta percha in his hands as he did so, he realised that he had made a golf ball.

Picture his excitement as he teed up his invention, took out his driver—and hit a miserable, scuttling shot of the type familiar to anyone who has ever hit a modern ball a glancing blow on the top, known to addicts as an egg-opener.

How many great inventions have resulted from some tiny circumstance of fate. What, for instance, prompted Archimedes to take that historic bath? A pointed remark, possibly, from a near and dear one. And if a summer shower had driven Newton in from the orchard before the apple dropped, it might have been years before the world received the Newton pippin, not to mention that scientific thing.

In the case of our professor, the fateful fluke which was to alter the entire nature of golf and pave the way for Arnold Palmer's private jet airliner, was the fact that the parsimonious academic was not a very good golfer. Had he been a scratch man his reaction to that first, unsatisfactory scuffle with a gutta percha ball would have been, 'That's no good. Ah well, it was worth a try!'

As it was he persevered in the belief that perhaps his shot had been at fault. So did others. They discovered that the longer they played with gutta percha balls the better the results. Students of aerodynamics will need no further explanation. A perfectly smooth sphere makes a poor missile. But as the gutta percha balls became roughened by the impact of clubs, they responded to lift caused by eddying air over the indentations and flew far and straight. Players experimented by hammering different patterns on their gutties to discover the most effective arrangement. The professionals quickly moved in. One manufacturer produced gutties to resemble the familiar feathery, complete with moulded seams and stitches; he must have been an ancestor of the man who invented the plastic tomato ketchup container. Others tried lattice-work and bramble patterns and it was not until long after the introduction of the rubber-cored ball that golf ball makers discovered the most effective arrangement of dimples which is used universally today.

Quite a mystique grew up around the gutties which were available in five sizes, according to drachm weight. Strong men went for the 29 which had the advantage that when it became mis-shapen and had to be remoulded it still made a decent sized ball. (Balls lost a proportion of their material in play through chipping, and extra gutta percha could not be added satisfactorily in the remoulding process.) Willie Park of Musselburgh, the first of the philosopher-scientist breed of professional golfers, recommended that in selecting gutties care should be taken to ensure that they were at least six months old but not much older. They should, he said, be good 'stotters'—giving a high bounce with a clear hard click when dropped on a flagstone—and the loss of elasticity in play meant it wasn't worthwhile remaking them a second time.

I have never played with a feathery. Those that have survived

are museum pieces and even if one could get hold of a few, they
would be quite unplayable today. One blow would split 100-year-
old leather. But I have handled them enough to get an idea of how
they performed. My colleague Pat Ward-Thomas, golf correspondent of *The Guardian*, played a fair amount with a sort of feathery
in a German prisoner-of-war camp. They could not get golf balls
and so the Stalag Open had to be played with a hand-stitched ball.
The feathery was not all that inferior; drives of 200 yards and more
were recorded with it in favourable conditions. However, I *have*
played with the gutty and I think I can appreciate something of the
stir its arrival must have caused. It feels hard and 'stoney' to hands
accustomed to the rubber ball but it goes almost as far as its
modern counterparts when hit solidly off the meat of the clubhead
and it is distinctly better to putt with.

Not everyone welcomed the gutty at first. Old pros, who were
also ball makers, tried to protect their vested interests by deriding
the new fangled gutty and they received some support, as always
when innovation is on the wind, from those who were tempera-
mentally dedicated to the old fangled as a matter of principle. The
resistance movement didn't prevail for long against the gutty's
clear advantages and golf was emancipated, free to develop in
subtleties of skill never before possible.

The job of assessing just how good the early golfers were is
difficult, futile and booby-trapped with hidden fallacies. It is perhaps only apt to say that the gutty opened up the first golden age
of golf and that the giants of those days—the Morrises and the
Parks—were very considerable players. Willie Park of Musselburgh and Tom Morris of Prestwick shared the first five Opens—
the championship which was inaugurated in 1860—but by their
own admission they were no match for their sons. The romantic
young Tom was, by contemporary consensus, the peer of them all.
He won four successive Opens and would have added to his tally
but the death of his wife broke him and he himself died soon
afterwards, before he was thirty and before his brilliant golf career
had reached full flowering.

Willie Park junior is shabbily treated in the record books. He won two Opens and was by common consent the outstanding putter of his day. Ironically, he lost a third Open through missing a short putt but stroke play was not his forte. He excelled as a match player and maintained a regular challenge to all comers, £50 a side, in the advertisement columns of the golfing press and made a very good thing out of it until the opposition began to recognise the truth of his motto 'a good putter is a match for anyone'.

For the first thirty years of the Open Championship one prediction could be made about the winner with certainty; he would be a Scot. Although the game had been carried south and across the Atlantic to the New World (the first American club was formed in Charleston as early as 1786) Scotland was the game's powerhouse and its citizens, wherever they lived, were the master race.

In those early days the gap in playing standards between pro and amateur was nothing like so pronounced as it was later to become. A gentleman of substance who became bitten by the golf bug could devote as much time as he cared to his new pursuit. For their part the pros in the main were a feckless breed of individuals who lived largely by caddying and from what they could win in wagers. They were probably not as good golfers as they might have been and, as one Scottish pro put it, the only difference he could see between amateur and pro was that 'the amateur gets mair to eat and mair to drink'. So far as the second part of that definition is concerned, history records many examples of notable exceptions; golf has never been a teetotal game.

The era of Scottish supremacy ended in 1890 and its downfall was achieved by two amateurs. Convention demands that they be formally styled, Mr. John Bell and Mr. Harold Hilton. The amateur championships of those years were dominated by a few outstanding players. Apart from Mr. Ball and Mr. Hilton, there were Mr. Horace Hutchinson, who was also a prolific and wonderful writer on the game, Mr. John Lindlay, and Mr. Freddie Tait, a dashing and brilliant young golfer who was killed as a lieutenant of the Black Watch in the Boer War.

Mr. Ball and Mr. Hilton both won Open Championships and the extent of the eclipse of Scottish golf can be measured from the fact that, with the single exception of Willie Auchterlonie's victory in 1893, no home-based Scot has ever won an Open since. But if amateurs forced the break it was professionals from England who turned it into a rout. The balance of power tipped decisively towards the south with the arrival of three men who were known, with heavy Victorian whimsy, as the Great Triumvirate.

J. H. Taylor learned his golf as a caddie at Westward Ho! This fine Devonshire links gave young Taylor a thorough grounding in the arts of seaside golf and playing in wind but a stronger influence was the inspiration of Horace Hutchinson. Taylor worked for a time as a bootboy in the Hutchinson household and he recalls in his autobiography how he gave an extra spit and polish to the 'tacketty boots' of his hero.

Harry Vardon's introduction to the game was less formal. He began as a boy with a home-made club, pick-up balls and an obsessional enthusiasm. He even laid out his own course on the Channel Island linksland near his home because he and his friends were not allowed on the proper course. His expertise and the quality of his equipment gradually improved. Right from the beginning, then, he had to find his own solutions to the problems of hitting a golf ball and this, I suspect, was the secret of his subsequent success. All good judges who saw Vardon in his prime agreed that he had raised the standards of play to a level never seen before. His method, uniquely his own but quickly adopted as the universal *ne plus ultra* of style, was created by a process of experiment, rejection and refinement and owed nothing to principles of conventional teaching. When Vardon came along golfers had to accept that everyone before then, to a greater or lesser extent, had been swinging the club wrong.

Today Vardon's name is mainly celebrated in the Vardon Grip, the method used by 99 per cent of golfers to hold the clubs, with the little finger of the right hand overlapping the first two fingers of the left. In fact, although Vardon used this grip, he did not, contrary to popular legend, invent it. The advantages of this method had been known and applied by many players. Vardon, who had discovered independently the superiority of an overlapping grip can only be said to have popularized this technique. My opinion, for what it is worth, is that the virtues of the Vardon Grip are exaggerated. Jack Nicklaus (interlocking) and Dai Rees (two-handed, or baseball grip) are witnesses to unconventional methods. I suspect that many golfers, specially longer handicap players whose hands are small and weak, would benefit from a change to unorthodoxy.

The third member of the Triumvirate was James Braid, an eminent Scot whose name will always be associated with Walton Heath, in my view one of the greatest inland courses to be found anywhere in the world. The public first began to take notice of this unknown club-maker from the Army and Navy Stores when he held the champion, Taylor, to a half in an exhibition match. They were to hear plenty more of him. Between them these three men won 16 Open Championships in twenty-one years. (Vardon 6, Taylor 5, Braid 5). But more significant than the number of their victories was the manner of their winning. For the first time the big guns of the golfer's armoury were used as implements as much of accuracy as distance. The Triumvirate expected to hit their fairway woods close to the flag and they had the skill to encourage such tactics.

It was this which really marked the era of the Triumvirate. The fact that these three had developed their skills in England rather than Scotland was coincidental. The real distinguishing factor was that they raised the standard of play, and set new targets for others to aim at, which had never been achieved before. For my money, this aspect of the Triumvirate was much more important than another change which is generally accepted as marking the start of the modern era of golf. Experiments with steel shafts had been pursued in a desultory fashion from as early as 1897. What is thought to be the first steel-shafted club is owned by W. S. Collins, professional at the North Wales club, Llandudno. He keeps it in his shop, fixed to the wall against the possibility of collector's fever proving stronger than golfing scruples, but kindly untethered it for me to waggle. The shaft is hexagonal in section and the blacksmith who made it got round the problem of the excessive weight by drilling as many holes as he could find room for in each face, a technique which is used by motor racing enthusiasts to reduce the weight of their cars. A full swing of this club is a ponderous and strenuous business and I could quite see that even a well-muscled blacksmith would have realised that his gift to golf wasn't quite ready. But this prototype did have one fascinating novelty. The rush of wind through all those perforations produced a loud whistling sound which must have struck terror into the heart of an opponent, much in the manner of sirens on the German JU87 dive-bombers during the Second World War. I rather regret that this aid to the psychological warfare of golf was lost in the development of more sophisticated steel shafts, which came into general use in the 1920's.

A rather more telling innovation was the rubber-cored ball. It was an American golfer, Coburn Haskell, who devised the method of winding rubber thread under tension around a solid centre and encasing it in a gutta percha cover. As with the gutty, the Haskell's arrival started a spirited controversy. The first rubber balls could not be driven noticeably farther than the gutty and many golfers thought them too lively for control. No one was more scathing about the inferior rubber interloper than Sandy Herd, a player whose place in golf history had already been secured by his advice to a noble but willowy pupil, 'Anchor your ass, my lord!' Having announced that he proposed to play a gutty for the 1904 Open he changed his mind after a last-minute practice, switched to a Haskell and won it by a single stroke from Vardon who had remained faithful to the gutty. Sneaky, perhaps, but convincing. Discussion of the relative merits of the two varieties of ball ceased forthwith.

The war of 1914–18 ended the era of the Triumvirate and when competitive golf was resumed in 1919 the initiative had passed overseas. The change was neither dramatic nor immediately apparent. The first appearance of the Americans Jim Barnes and Walter Hagen, at the Deal Open of 1920, raised no eyebrows. Barnes came sixth, Hagen nowhere, and as far as British golf was concerned God was still in His heaven and all was right with the world.

The following year, however, there occurred at St. Andrews an event to test the inflexibility of the British upper lip. Jock Hutchison, playing out of the Glenview Club, Chicago, won the Open. True he was only a made-over American, having been decently born and raised in Scotland, but the cup went overseas for only the second time in its existence. (Arnaud Massy, the Basque, whom legend has endowed with prodigious power, won it in 1907.) Britain could take no comfort from technicalities of birth when the next Open came to be played. The winner at Sandwich, Walter Hagen, was as American as bootleg liquor and, with his colourful appearance and brash personality, scarcely less palatable to British tastes. A foreigner—and an outsider at that! Hagen never changed but the natives did; they came to regard this raffish adventurer as a favourite relative for whom allowances must be made.

During the nineteenth century and the early part of the twentieth, the gospel of golf had been carried to every corner of the earth, mainly by missionaries from Scotland. A hole at Carnoustie is named after the experience of one such emigrant. This worthy set off for the New World and he had gone no farther than the end of the golf course when he fell down in a drunken stupor. He awoke under the impression that his journey was complete and the hole is known as South America to this day. (He never tried again; he built a cottage and lived in Carnoustie for the rest of his life although this small village exported more than a hundred teachers of golf.)

The golfing chickens which had been carried abroad by those pioneers now began to come home to roost in ever increasing measure. American golf historians generally date the ending of the British era rather earlier. For their purposes the U.S. Open

Championship of 1913 at Brookline, Mass., marked the watershed. The favourites were Vardon and another Englishman, Ted Ray, who were on a tour of the United States.

To the delighted astonishment of the American sporting public an unknown teenager, Francis Ouimet, a sporting-goods salesman who had to be ordered by his boss to play in the championship, tied with Ray and Vardon after four rounds with a score of 304. The excitement when Ouimet calmly won the play-off can be imagined. Certainly this famous victory gave an enormous impetus to American golf, although I do not accept that it was the starting-point of overseas supremacy. I see it as the first swallow possibly, not the first day of summer. Vardon was by then past his prime and fatigued from his tour. And the U.S. Open at that time was nothing like as important as it later became; it could in no sense be regarded as a world championship in 1913 as the British Open could (and still can).

If the timing of the revolution admits of some argument, the comprehensive nature of it does not. Hagen, Barnes, Jones, Armour, Shute, Saracen and Snead took it in turns to humiliate British golf. The Open Championship Cup spent less than three months in Britain during a ten-year period, just long enough to be put up for competition and handed back into American safekeeping.

The home professionals reasserted themselves briefly in the years before the Second World War, notably Henry Cotton, who had developed into a golfer of the highest international standing, but Hitler nipped this renaissance in the bud.

The post-war years belonged to the commonwealth. Bobby Locke, the South African who was felicitously described as walking the fairways like an archbishop's butler at the beginning of a tournament and like the archbishop himself at the end, carried all before him with a god-like putting action and the coolest golfing brain of his, and possibly anyone else's, time.

The Americans, at this period, had ceased to enter the Open in such strength as previously—they had fatter fish to fry at home—but I do not think that this should be held to detract from Locke's achievement. In his heyday he was assuredly a match for any contemporary. The same stipulation must be applied to the five Opens of Peter Thomson, the Australian whose disciplined, three-quarter powered swing must be ranked among the nearest challengers to a perfect realisation of the theoretical potential of transferring human energy into the swift, straight flight of a golf ball.

This period was the only time in the modern history of golf that the progress of the game was not faithfully reflected in the shiny contours of the Open Championship Cup. Great events were stirring in America. Bobby Jones, to my mind unquestionably the greatest golfer of all time, dwarfed his contemporaries and when he retired there was a temporary waning of public interest.

But his going eventually stimulated competition—as he knew it would. I'm sure that thought influenced Jones's decision to quit. Quite simply it gave someone else a chance to win. The pros had something to work for now that they had to compete against ordinary mortals. This comforting assurance was to be shaken from time to time. Byron Nelson, an artist at 'working' the ball with sidespin to gain an advantage from wind and slope, won thirteen tournaments in succession. And Ben Hogan conceived the ambition to become a perfect golfing machine. He applied himself to this notion with intelligence and dedication and he might have succeeded. A car crash robbed him of the prime years and although he fought back to the point where his brother professionals acknowledged him to be the finest striker of them all, his suspect putting prevented him from realizing his full potential.

Although at the time of writing we are possibly too close to the recent past to see events in their true perspective, I am prepared to recognize the rise of a new golfing era in the late nineteen-fifties. We can call it the era of the giants or the era of the common man, both are equally appropriate. Either way, it began with the partnership of Arnold Palmer and Mark McCormack.

The question of whether Palmer is a good golfer is open to discussion. (Good, that is, in the context of the most illustrious players of all time. In the everyday sense of the term he is, of course, a very good golfer.) But that he is a great golfer there can be no doubt.

The key to Palmer's success, it seems to me, is to be found in two parts of his personality which psychiatrists would doubtless regard as signs of immaturity. He is impelled by an overwhelming desire to be cock of the walk, to prove himself to be best. And he is a gambler; if he can see a half chance he will go for it boldly. There is more to him than that but these are the essentials in his temperament that set him apart as a golfer. On the one hand they often make up for deficiencies in his game; he has no peer at turning disaster into triumph in one bold stroke. And at the same time they make him an outstandingly exciting golfer to watch.

McCormack, an acute and perceptive lawyer, exploited this promising new material and created a giant. He elevated Palmer to a status that no sportsman—unless you include bullfighters and thereby degrade the name of sport—had enjoyed before. The Palmer legend, assiduously nourished both by image-building techniques and doughty deeds on the course, fired a worldwide golfing explosion.

Enthusiasm for golf in Japan, for instance, turned into a national hysteria. Land is scarce in a highly condensed country like Japan and so the only release for the urge to golf for thousands of Japanese is in multi-storey driving ranges. And for all too many of them, this is the only form of the game they will ever know. To get into some clubs you have to be wealthy, socially O.K., and be put down for membership at birth. In England and America you may have to start queuing at two in the morning if you want to play a municipal course on Sunday morning but you do eventually set foot on real grass.

Japan is an extreme case but there are few places where golf is not played and growing day by day. The plant has not withered entirely in the Communist world and there are signs of new growth in Czechoslovakia, Yugoslavia, Bulgaria and Rumania. Today it is no longer a rich man's game. Devotees must be counted in millions and the major problem of the game is to provide facilities for all the new recruits who are looking for somewhere to play.

On the professional level the game has become a major spectator sport (some fifty million people watch the U.S. Open and the Masters on television) and the stars of this great industry earn as much as their fellow entertainers in Hollywood. Most golfers watch the new developments in the game with mixed feelings. Not all the changes are welcomed without reserve by all.

A large measure of the praise and the blame for our brave new golfing world must be directed at Palmer and McCormack. And if there are bits of it that we don't like, we can at least take comfort from the broad view that the game is in a healthier state today than at any time in its royal and ancient history.

2

Our mother, that sad old bitch

IT was a matter of historical accident that decreed that a round of golf should be played over eighteen holes. In the early days of the game's development there was no standard number of holes. The available land was the governing factor. Holes were laid out according to convenience on the linkland, the waste common ground which bordered the sea. Some courses could accommodate nine holes only, others fourteen or more. It so happened that at St. Andrews the players found it convenient to hole out eighteen times as they played out to the farthest promontory of their narrow strip of links and returned, using the same greens in many cases, to the starting-point. And as St. Andrews developed as the most influential centre of the game so eighteen holes became accepted as the norm.

The reputation of the Old Course also set the standards for golf course layout and even today there are people who believe that links golf is not just the best but indeed the only true form of the game. It is a point of view with which I have little patience. Apart from the selfishness of denying that those who play inland are real golfers, it ignores the fact that golf is developing. New equipment has changed the game entirely and, in any case, St. Andrews is no longer the course it used to be. This part of the coast of Fife is subject to silting and whereas the Old Course used to be right alongside the shore it is now nearly a mile inland. Changes in the character of the turf have been largely accelerated by modern techniques of course management. Artificial fertilisers have enriched (and coarsened the grass) and automatic water-

29

sprinklers have softened the greens. These innovations have been introduced in the name of progress but the result, in my opinion, has been the destruction of the Old Course. Instead of being a monument to the pioneers of the game, St. Andrews today is an unhappy mixture. The matriarch of golf has been tarted up in lipstick and mini-skirt. The dignity of antiquity has been lost and her character compromised. She is a sad old bitch of a golf course, grotesquely old fashioned by modern standards and hopelessly raddled to those who loved her as she was. The city of St. Andrews is established as the home of golf and is the Mecca of enthusiasts from every corner of the world. The city fathers are conscious of their responsibility to the past and to the present, but in my view their compromising does a gross disservice to both.

How much more satisfactory it would be if they let the Old Course revert to as near her original condition as nature allowed. Take away the automatic-sprinklers and allow the greens to become as hard and fast as glass. Let the fairways be so that once again a golfer might be able, as the American Craig Wood once did, see his drive kick into a bunker some 400 yards distant down the wind. And, for good measure, provide pencil-case quivers of hickory clubs so that visitors could get an idea, if a sketchy one, of what the game was like during the genesis of golf. In other words, make St. Andrews a living museum.

But what of the modern game? From time to time one hears enlightened legislators talk of a national golf course and there could be no more appropriate location for a Scottish national course than St. Andrews. I would like to see the city join forces with their distinguished tenants, the R. & A., in amalgamating the New and Jubilee courses into one championship course built to the best modern standards. Here we get into difficult country for there is no commonly accepted formula for what constitutes a good course. One player may like a hole because he can play it well, while another finds a hole 'good' on account of its difficulty. And what to a big hitter is an easy par is often an impossibility to the novice, specially if a water carry is involved. Yet if certain principles are followed, it is possible to build holes which provide a good test for good and bad players alike.

My first requirement in a golf hole is that it shall set a problem even before the player selects a club on the tee. He should, in fact, be faced with a number of options and be forced to balance potential advantages against possible dangers. On straightforward par-four holes there should be a basic route which offers a par (even for the long-handicap man making use of his stroke) without any exceptional difficulty. And then there should be at least one alternative way in for the gambler who is prepared to flirt with disaster in the hopes of making a birdie. Sheer length should never be the sole criterion. The reward should be balanced by danger so that the big-hitter who misses the line is penalized for his error. This does not necessarily mean bottlenecked fairways; a long drive allows less margin for error anyway, but the hazards in the long-hitter's target area should be severe enough to make him think twice before chancing his arm. In the American Open Championship of 1967 at Baltusrol, New Jersey, an exceptionally dry spell had left the rough so thin that Jack Nicklaus was able to aim into it deliberately at some holes. His immense strength gave him a disproportionate advantage that week and although he was a worthy winner, his less powerful rivals were never in with a chance. I have mentioned only two possibilities but of course cunning architects can devise holes which offer many tactical possibilities. But basically the par-four green should be within the scope of two good but unexceptional shots, or a safe tee shot and an outstanding second, or a marvellous drive followed by a relatively easy approach.

The problems of a good golf hole may often be entirely psychological. The tenth hole at Sunningdale is a good example. It is a par four and well within range for most players. The fairway is wide enough to accommodate a football pitch and the vast green slopes benignly to hold the second shot. It looks seductively easy and therein lies its subtle dangers. For you drive from the crest of a ridge and that vast expanse of fairway falling below you imparts a powerful exhilaration. Standing on that tee you feel that you could hit the ball a mile. The temptation to give your drive that little bit extra is irresistible. You let fly and, wide as the fairway is, it is not so generous as to accommodate the resulting hook or slice. The Sunningdale woods are carpeted with the composting remnants of cards torn up at this hole. No wonder they have a refreshment hut behind that green; if ever there was a place where a golfer needed a restorative it is here.

Most courses have siren holes where the trouble is provided in the imagination of the player and frequently they involve water. Quite a modest carry across a pond can undo normally stout-hearted players. I once played with a distinguished Fleet Street editor who topped five balls in succession into the pond off the tee although he was quite capable of making the carry with a five iron. When we came to that hole in the afternoon he solemnly approached the water's edge and threw a new ball, still in its wrapper, into the pond. 'That's to appease the water devil,' he said, and with his private devil duly exorcised, he played a splendid tee shot safely and far up the fairway.

Another psychological hole is to be found at the Mid Ocean Club in Bermuda. Like the tenth at Sunningdale the tee is elevated and you have to drive across the corner of a bay. Here greed is the gremlin. If you are content with a modest drive it is an easy shot. But the more water you can carry the easier the second shot and avarice too often gets the better of discretion. And even if you hit a Sunday Special exactly on the line you have chosen, it frequently falls short of dry land simply because of the deceptive nature of the view. Shots from elevated tees always, but always, fall twenty yards short of where you expect.

Another hole which deserves a place in any discussion about the psychological problems of golf is the thirteenth at Estoril. Again an elevated tee distorts the player's view of the situation for it looks driveable although, in practice, only the very best tee shot will be anywhere near the green. Further illusory difficulties are provided by the boundaries because this hole is built on a strip of land connecting the two main areas of the course and there are out-of-bounds walls on both sides of the fairway. And, what's more, these walls converge to form a tight-looking bottleneck at about the 160-yard mark. The prospect is made more forbidding by trees beyond the bottleneck on the right, bushes on the left and a vast bunker in the middle.

Standing on that tee the tactical thought suggests itself with hypnotic force that the only shot is to hit a big one past this gauntlet of trouble and reach the comparatively ample expanse in front of the green. This auto-suggestion is accompanied by a stern warning that the shot must be absolutely straight to avoid the out-of-bounds (thus introducing a nervous factor which greatly increases the probability of a bad shot) and it must be given a bit extra in the way of power (thus virtually guaranteeing a bad shot).

During the Portuguese Open Championship of 1968, I stood behind this green and revelled in the misfortunes of the competitors, having suffered grievously myself here earlier in the week. I watched one player hit seven balls out-of-bounds—these were pros and low handicap amateurs—and in the space of half an hour no-one managed to achieve the par of four. They walked off that green with the dazed expression of soldiers who had come up against a secret weapon, sadly marking sixes, sevens and eights on their cards and looking back pensively at the monster.

I walked back up the hole to analyse its terrors and concluded that they were entirely imaginary. At its narrowest point the fairway, which looks from the tee as wasp-waisted as an Edwardian beauty, is a voluptuous forty yards wide. As a par four it is a pushover if you play a mid-iron to the green. If ... there's the rub. The terrible twins of golf, fear and greed, are irresistible on that tee—fears of the dangers and greed for the chance of an easy-looking birdie. This hole represents for me the ultimate in one of course architecture's most important aspects, a major challenge in tactics combined with a reward for the player who finds the right solution, and has the resolution to achieve it without exceptional length or accuracy. The main consideration is that virtuosity should

C

be rewarded and impetuosity punished. This thought brings me to my second requirement in a golf hole and that is the need to get what you hit. The golfing term 'rub of the green' has a fine sporting flavour about it and yet it is one of the most contentious phrases in golf. The traditionalists believe that luck, both good and bad, is an essential ingredient and that the buffeting of fortune tests the character of a man no less than his skill. To me this attitude is poppycock. I can see little virtue in a man maintaining a stoic calm at the sight of his perfectly-struck drive bouncing wildly from the centre of a fairway into the rough. In such circumstances he is entitled to be upset. There is enough luck involved in playing on the most beautifully-fashioned fairways without that sort of non-sense which makes a mockery of golf and reduces it to the chancy level of playing a pin-table machine. I have heard venerable members at venerable clubs declare with pride that in certain conditions it is not humanly possible to hold a fairway. My private reaction on these occasions is that it would be best to get to work on that sacred turf with a bulldozer. And while they had the machine at their disposal they would be well advised to remove the obstructions at the blind holes. For to the dictum that a golfer should get what he hits I would add the rider that he should see what he is trying to hit.

Of course there is also a danger of going too far in the opposite direction and this is specially the case in the United States. Many American courses are prepared with lush fairways and greens the consistency of fudge so that the delicate arts of the game are rendered unnecessary. There is no call to 'work' the ball with fade or draw, to run up, or flight the ball low. A standard straight shot followed by a pitch that plops into the green and stops dead, or even spins back towards the player, is all that is necessary.

Golf offers a vast variety of holes covering 700-yard slogs across American pastures, flick-with-a-wedge holes to greens which are browns, simply areas of sand which have been flattened and oiled, in the Middle East, and mountain holes in Central Europe which are almost perpendicular. At Semmering in Austria there is a short hole where you have to crane forward over the front of the tee and look almost vertically downward to see the green. Then you let your gaze travel upward to mark the line on a distant peak. It is the only hole I know which seriously suggests that you tee up the ball and play your putter.

For all this rich diversity, all golf holes can be divided by character into four categories: those that look easy and are; those that look easy and aren't; those that look difficult but aren't and those that look difficult and are. A good course has a mixture of all four types and the aim of the design should be to produce a course which rings the psychological changes throughout a round. The mood and tempo must vary and beyond that generalisation, all I would add is that the first hole should be easy (to avoid a traffic jam when there are many matches waiting to start) and the last hole should be a real stinker.

Unless he has an unlimited budget and can command mountains to be created, the architect's task is largely dictated by the natural terrain. The general standard of golf course design is extremely high and although some designers sign their work with an unmistakable personal autograph, the best of them are like cosmetic surgeons. Their greatest triumphs look like happy accidents of nature and appear to have simply grown that way without help of man.

Not the least of golf's attractions is that it is played in beautiful surroundings. Courses are nice places to be. But God and the architect cannot do it all. The player himself must bring the proper state of mind with him to a golf course. If the golfer arrives late, rushes into the locker-room and comes to the first tee in a mental turmoil, his game will suffer and, in doing so, he will not appreciate the surroundings. He will lose on two counts, in the score and in aesthetic enjoyment for he will hardly see the scenery at all. A leisurely preparation for golf rewards the player doubly and is essential for getting the most out of the game.

If it is important to start a round of golf in the right mood it is even more vital to sustain it through the inevitable patches of disappointment. Unsatisfactory incidents are bound to happen, if only the missing of short putts. More important than preserving personal tranquillity at such moments is the duty not to upset other people. Their moods, too, are fragile and the rules of golf etiquette have been designed to eliminate all possible sources of friction. The attitude to take on to the golf course is to see yourself and all the other players as bottles of vintage port which should on no account be shaken. So while a golfer takes care not to disturb the sediment of his own temperament, he also offers the same consideration to others by not driving into them, or disturbing them with loud shouts of glee or anger, or holding them up by slow play, or leaving a trail of unraked bunkers, gaping divots or ball-pocked greens. The spell of golfing enchantment is easily broken by thoughtless behaviour; all my memories of misery on the course concern ill-mannered behaviour by people in other matches rather than my own bad play. Don't shake the bottles.

In saying this I am only too aware that many British clubhouses do not tempt the visitor to linger. All too often the atmosphere is as cheerless as an old-fashioned railway waiting-room with the added disadvantage, in the locker room, of a musty smell compounded of unwashed clothing, dry rot and dust.

Very few clubhouses in Britain were built for the purpose. Many courses have been created from the parks of great estates. The club has naturally used the mansion as its headquarters and while the classical proportions of a Georgian masterpiece may present a picturesque and even imposing background to the eighteenth green, it is a sight to strike a chill to the marrow of a golfer's bones. As the tyres of my car crunch the gravel on the drives of such places, I am always reminded of a television advertisement which showed a drawing-room of baronial proportions whose floor was closely covered with oil heaters. A voice proclaimed: 'It would take 130 heaters (or 230 or some such nonsensical number) to warm this room. . . .' From experience I know that mansion clubhouses contain rooms just like this one and that you are lucky to find even one small heater or tepid radiator.

The magnificence of these houses depended on the fortunes of their owners and since golf clubs do not corner the East Indian tea market, or traffic in slaves, or even inherit vast lands settled on ancestors who earned the gratitude of their monarch as warriors or pimps, they cannot afford to keep up the expensive standards for which the houses were designed. Tawdriness and decay and discomfort are the order of the day. It is rather grand to think that the room where the trollies are stored was designed by Adam, or that Queen Elizabeth and a randy lord might once have mocked her title of the virgin queen upstairs in the card room. But historical associations make a poor salve for chilblains and ghosts cannot hide peeling paintwork. Clubs which took over houses of more modest pretensions fare better but conversions, however skilled, are never entirely satisfactory.

After the socially-degraded mansion, the other main category of clubhouse is the multiplying-cell variety. This occurs in cases where there was no building with the original land and the members started in a small way with a basic box. Over the years bits are added. As women are admitted, for instance, a room is built on for them. Then perhaps another bar is tacked on to the structure. The servant problem requires that housing accommodation be provided for a resident steward and this is attached. Then a committee room, a secretary's office, pro's shop. . . . The history of the club is reflected in the graduations of the brickwork of the rambling building. The process, although inevitable, is unsatisfactory. And it is aggravated by the nature of clubs. One club, for instance, reached the point where a further expansion was necessary and co-opted a special committee consisting of no less than eight architects from the membership. With a committee of laymen there is always a chance that one dominant personality may impose his will and thus avoid the worst excesses of compromise. But eight experts!

Finance is the over-riding consideration in clubhouse architecture and the question of what ought to be done is always governed by the limitations of how much money is available. Golf in Britain is cheap, in Scotland excessively so. It is the game's most valued tradition. Club members lose no opportunity to tell each other, and the committee, that subscriptions are too high. And when the disease of creeping inflation makes a rise in subs inevitable, there are always men willing to martyr themselves on the pyre of resignation rather than pay another five pounds a year. They die, as golfers, in the sacred cause of cheap golf. Others honour the tradition by slandering the committee. It is a safe bet that at any time of the day or night in some golf clubs in some part of the world, a florid-faced member is slopping his gin and tonic in emphatic diatribe: 'If the Greens/House/Entertainments Committee ran their business the way they ran this Club they'd go broke in a week. They could *halve* the subs if only they had the sense to . . . .'

Subscriptions are based on an estimate of what it will cost to run the club for a year. That figure, divided by the number of members, produces the amount which the sub *has* to be. Nobody bothered seriously to ask whether the amount was economically reasonable because the question was irrelevant. What must be must be. What *ought* to be is beside the point.

When Lilley Brook golf club at Cheltenham decided that they needed a new clubhouse the committee had no very clear idea of what it should be like. They called in a firm of architects and if events had run their usual course there would have followed a succession of discussions on the relative merits of exposed beams and weathered brick, Cotswold stone, untreated pine panelling and wipe-down plastics. And the lobbying over whether hip-baths should be preferred to showers or whether a committee room was more important than a ladies' lounge can be imagined. The one undisputed fact was that it must not cost more than £22,000.

Mr. Roger Dyer, the partner responsible for the project, neatly side-stepped the labyrinth of committee argument by pointing out that no-one had ever properly determined the precise function of a golf club. What is a golf club? What is its function? How can a building best serve this purpose? When these fundamental questions have been answered we can begin to think about planning on a rational basis.

OUR MOTHER, THAT SAD OLD BITCH

The questions may seem to be so basic as to be obvious. But as we have seen in the case of club-makers who lost sight of the elementary question: 'What is the function of a golf club?', so planners had been working in the dark in the matter of buildings. The kind of information which was needed was the number of showers necessary per hundred members, the area required for a trolley park, how many thermal units are consumed in the drying of 100 saturated sweaters. Hard, practical stuff which had previously been tackled by rule of thumb or, more often, by rule of cheque book.

A questionnaire circulated among clubs supplied few answers; there was little sign of conformity and the overall result was simply to reinforce the need for reliable figures. Detailed studies were made and revealed, for instance, that many clubs had locker rooms which were wastefully large. On the basis of a fourball going off every six minutes for three hours, plus a bit of leeway to accommodate overlapping, an eighteen-hole course can take a maximum of 150 players. At any one time, therefore, the locker room is occupied by far fewer people than most clubs cater for. Mr. Dyer planned accordingly (four square feet of floor per locker) with a considerable saving of cash and space over the usual provision.

This type of information was valuable, if dull, and the research was all part of the routine homework which an architect undertakes in designing a building. One of golf's most intractable problems was solved during this preliminary work. The spikes of golf shoes quickly destroy most of the usual forms of floor covering; they are almost as bad as the stilletto heels of women's shoes which became a fashionable rage during the sixties. It was found that the rubber belting used to operate the massive winding-wheels at coal mines made an ideal and indestructible cover for locker-room gangways, non-slip, non-sounding and non-penetrating.

The next and far more significant planning phase, was to decide what we may call the philosophic concept of a golf club. What, in fact, is it? Mr. Dyer's answer to this question was simple and heretical. A golf club, he pronounced, is simply a pub plus locker rooms. Holding up a damp finger into the wind of social change, and guided by his experience of golf in America, he decided that the trend must be towards a comprehensive country club. The entire family must be catered for, not just father's golf. He reasoned that a golf club has to have kitchens, dining-room, bars and locker rooms. If golf alone were involved none of these expensive amenities could be used to capacity and so justify their capital cost. The plant must be used fully.

By adopting the conception of the golf club as a pub, the prospect opened of a building which could be fully operational all day and, even more important, all evening. Instead of being an expensive liability, the kitchens and bars could be the main source of income and profit. Mr. Dyer knew from experience in the hotel and brewing industries that a sympathetic environment plus a friendly barman plus a cash register was a certain formula for creating a private mint. An outlay of £11,000 on an attractive interior design so transformed one pub, for instance, that its gross income multiplied sevenfold. In another case clever interior design resulted in a gross weekly turnover of £800 for a one-room discotheque.

Why shouldn't golf clubs dip their bread into this rich gravy? They could, if they put their minds to it, according to Mr. Dyer's thesis. Why not a large social membership who would use the club as a restaurant and pub as well as for dances, bingo, films or any other activity? Anything to keep the plant profitably occupied. Tennis, squash, swimming, archery, riding—all this sort of thing would help to involve whole families and make the club a comprehensive leisure centre. And the increased profits from bar and dining-room would mean that the golfer's subscription could be reduced. That tonic thought is probably enough to overcome the stuffiest of objections to teenage rave-ups in the mixed bar and baccarat in the committee room.

At all events, the members of Lilley Brook were convinced of the soundness of the idea. And when they got their new clubhouse, what they had for their £22,000 was the nucleus of a country club complex with provision for future expansion into swimming, tennis and possibly motel-type weekend cottages.

All this, of course, is old hat in America where the country club is a strongly-entrenched institution. And, as everyone knows, the subscriptions are astronomic. Many of them require new members to buy bonds, running into thousands of dollars. However, as driving-range operators found out, it is not always possible to relate American institutions to British conditions. And if a club has enough well-to-do people in its catchment area, finance becomes secondary; it can afford to use the subscription as a weapon to regulate the social exclusivity of the membership, in the way that British Chancellors of the Exchequer adjust the excise duty on spirits to preserve the O.K. status of cirrhosis of the liver. Some American country clubs ensure a satisfactory income from bar and dining-room by requiring members to buy an annual quota of vouchers which can only be spent in the club.

Swinley Forest, the delightful club near Ascot in Berkshire, used to operate a variant of this system. At the end of the year they added up what it had cost to run the club and the members were duly informed how much they were required to pay. Two world wars gave successive governments an excuse to throw up their hands in despair and ignore Mr. Micawber's doctrine that annual income of one pound with annual expenditure of nineteen and six meant happiness. In its place both political parties have twisted the morals of Robin Hood into a political philosophy: steal from the rich and throw it away. The compulsory paupering of the nation put an end to Swinley Forest's haphazard ways; these days to operate such a system a club would have to be comprised entirely of tax-dodging swindlers, exactly the type who would never in any circumstances be allowed into Swinley.

Times are hard. Golf clubs must trim their standards to the economic winds and obtain revenue from any and every source. A fruit machine in the bar is not enough and green fees from visiting societies is like morphia, relieving the pain temporarily but without effecting a cure. Not that societies are A Bad Thing, far from it. The secretary of one southern club once told me through clenched teeth of a society which brought its own food and drink in their coach and spent nothing in the club. That sort of behaviour is exceptional. At the other end of the scale, the Irish Medical Golf Society has a reputation of enormous exuberance. After one of their visits the treasurer of a famous club was observed standing amid the wreckage of the bar, reading the till-roll and chuckling.

Societies are an important part of golf. They enable golfers to play on courses which they might otherwise never have the chance to visit, they are normally conducted in a refreshing Sunday school outing atmosphere and they make a significant contribution to the economics of club golf. Most people if asked to describe their most enjoyable day's golf would recall a society outing.

These days societies more and more provide the only opportunity for some members to play on a proper golf course at all. Around the major cities the pressure on private clubs is so great that waiting-lists of five years are not uncommon. The capital cost of building new courses is so large as to virtually rule out private enterprise. Municipal authorities are at last coming round to the view that public courses, far from representing a disproportionate outlay for a minority amenity, can be highly profitable sources of income. Even so, the expansion of golf in England has far outstripped the capacity of existing courses. At municipal courses near London a round at the weekend can only be had by queuing long before the dawn or by the luck of the draw in a postal ballot. With hardships of this order to surmount it is hardly surprising that many would-be golfers abandon their ambition and take up hobbies of a more available nature. Others who are less easily deflected have had to make do with forms of substitute golf which have sprung up in post-war years to cater for course starvation.

The phenomenal success of driving ranges in America suggested that the same thing might happen in Britain. The market was certainly ripe and the feeling was that all an entrepreneur needed was a field and a supply of golf balls and he could confidently start to plan for an early retirement in the West Indies. It didn't happen quite like that. Ranges were built without sufficient thought for the special British conditions, such as the fact that it rains quite often. Machines which happily picked up golf balls in the hard, dry conditions of California simply pressed them beyond recall into the Home Counties' mud. The expression 'sinking new capital' into golf ranges took on a sinister and literal meaning. Ranges were badly sited and casualties were high. And as a result the business earned an unfortunate reputation which was fostered by the tatty, run-down appearance of some of the survivors.

The blistered fingers of the pioneers served to warn later operators who came warily into the field. At this time, in the late sixties, the substitute-golf industry is just beginning to recover from its false start. Experience has shown that two categories of range are, to use the cant word of the moment, viable. The one-man business —just a field and a rudimentary shelter for the customers—is a working proposition and so is the golf centre, a comprehensive complex of range, par-three course, practice bunkers, putting greens, pitch-and-putt course and clubroom. There is scope for both types and I believe that now that the expensive lessons of the past have been assimilated we shall see a proliferation of both.

The word 'practice' is invested with unfortunate undertones. It conjures up miserable hours of Chopsticks at the piano and it offends against the English ideal of sportsmanship. The member of the friendly fourball who gets to the club half an hour early and hits a bucket of balls on the practice range is regarded as an oddity, if not an actual cad. The classical English sporting hero is, above all, casual. He cares nothing for appearances. The ultimate expression of correct sporting behaviour would be a man who is persuaded reluctantly to turn out for a cricket team, who arrived slightly late, borrowed some boots and a bat, strode to the wicket with flannels supported by a Greyhounds' tie and with his faded rowing-blue cap at a jaunty angle, hit a flowing century to snatch victory from disaster and then disappeared unobtrusively without waiting for the congratulations of his team mates.

When Roger Wethered tied for the 1921 Open Golf Championship his friends had to persuade him not to withdraw; he had promised to play for his village cricket team and didn't like to let them down by staying another day for the play-off. That's the spirit! It was said that Wethered's competitive fires did not seem to burn too fiercely in that play-off against Jock Hutchison. Of course not. By playing better than he expected, Wethered had put himself in the embarrassing position where he could not avoid letting the side down. There is, of course, no worse crime in the British public school code of morals. For the sake of golf history we must be grateful that cricket was the side he chose to betray when he was forced to the odious choice.

The traditional virtues have largely been superseded by the new morality but the remnants remain. The conditioning of boyhood still makes British professional golfers dress in drab camouflage which makes them invisible on the course. It is one of the reasons why they are at a disadvantage against their colourful and emancipated opponents from America. Golf is a game in which self-confidence is paramount. To look well is to feel well and to play well, but modesty prevents the British golfer from satisfying the peacock in his personality.

At club level the tradition is honoured even more strongly. Golfers wear clothes which are no longer respectable enough for gardening and any show of taking the game too seriously is thought to be un-English. Fortunately this attitude is under siege from the game's new recruits who did not have the disadvantage of a public school brainwashing but even so those who are anxious to improve their game by practice are often frustrated by lack of facilities.

That's where the ranges come in. Personally, I love going out in the evening to hit a bucket of balls into the night. It is a satisfying exercise if only as a release of the day's tensions and, if undertaken in a sensible manner, it can be extremely helpful for your game. Many range customers get carried away by their own instincts and, in an attempted reassurance of their manhood, try to hit every ball over the boundary fence. I am not competent to say whether such violence does indeed do anything for the psyche but as far as golf is concerned, all it achieves is to ingrain faults. The sensible golfing procedure is to fix a specific target for every shot, well within normal range, and decide exactly what type of shot is to be hit—straight, draw, fade, high or low. Start with short irons and take plenty of time between strokes in order for the mind and muscles to assimilate the lessons of every shot.

I am a believer in the theory that no shots are wasted. The golfer can learn as much if not more from bad shots as from good ones. There is a lot to be said for the technique of curing a slice by going to a range and deliberately trying to hit a slice. Practice positively. Firmly fix a purpose with every shot and, above all, *don't hit flat out*.

This is not to say that the player who takes his bucket of balls and slams into them 'belly, bum and bulging eyeballs' may not finish by hitting the ball like Gary Player. The satisfaction, I must warn, is transient. That superb tee shot never, but never, translates to the golf course. The sight of rough bordering the fairway tosses a psychological spanner into the works and inhibits the full-blooded swing of the previous evening. The result is spectacular and invariably spectacularly bad. So take it easy on the range and try, if possible, to 'play scared' as if on a real course.

3

March of the gladiators

THE world of tournament golf is the shop window of the game and as such it gives a glamorised picture of the merchandise. It is both sport and entertainment. Occasionally these functions become confused and tournament organizers try to emphasize the entertainment content with the techniques of showmanship. It never works. Entertainment arises from the sport, not the other way round, and so the finest spectaculars are produced by organizers whose interests are purely sporting. The Open Championships, run by national associations, seek only to provide a stiff test which will produce a worthy champion. Their single-minded sporting approach never fails to produce fine entertainment. On the other hand some commercial sponsors, who are mainly interested in getting the maximum publicity mileage out of their investment and who trick up their events and choose easy arenas in the hope of course-record headlines, often find themselves with a turkey on their hands. Paradoxes make hard learning.

For all that, life on the tournament circuits has a close affinity with the circus. The same nucleus of itinerant performers—plus a few new hopefuls and minus a few failures—moves on each week. The backstage staff of officials, caterers and pressmen goes with them, on to the same tents and the same routine. Long-running poker games are continued in a succession of hotels; so too are the feuds and the friendships. It is a mobile village with a life and a language of its own. And, like the circus, the enclosed world of tournament golf is slightly artificial. This remoteness from reality affects the players and many of them feel it to an oppressive degree

46

when they are off form. Slumped in the locker room after a bad score men who are envied by millions wonder if their lives have any meaning at all. What does it *matter*, when people are starving and shooting each other? It is a natural enough reaction and a most destructive thought for a professional golfer.

For the spectators a golf tournament is excitement. To the insiders it is frequently rather dull. The two sides have different terms of reference. The fan is looking for a winner in a gladiatorial contest; the players, apart from the few who are in contention, are earning a living. To them the glory of winning is a pleasant bonus but the main objective is income. Professional golf is hard work and often enough, when a man is out of the money and is simply going through the formality of completing the tournament at the end of the field, dreary work at that.

Millions of words have been written about the tensions of competitive golf and I do not propose to add much to the quota. The pressures affect golfers differently according to their temperaments. The spectator can imagine what it feels like to have a six-foot putt for a twenty thousand-dollar prize but he can never know. You have to do it. I have tried to get something of an insight into the feelings of the professional by playing in championships but it is impossible for an amateur to reproduce the situation, even approximately. When Lee Trevino, the Mexican American, teed up for the U.S. Open Championship in 1968 he was down and almost out. He had paid the entry fee with the last of his wife's savings. At the end of the week, as the winner, he was a millionaire. When he had 'that for the Open' it really was 'that' with a vengeance.

One result of my experience in big-time golf did surprise me. I was literally shaking with stage fright as I changed for my championship début and seriously doubted whether I would be able to hit the ball at all. But as I stepped on to the first tee my nervousness seemed to drain from my body; I looked at the spectators with their expressions of amused expectancy and became suffused with a feeling of arrogance. If these people were any good at this game, I thought, they would be on the tee with me, not gawping from the sidelines. I'll show them how it should be done. I was surprised at myself, for such an attitude is completely alien to my diffident nature.

It was almost as if I had been possessed. If so, I proved a satisfactory *doppelgänger* for I got away a decent enough shot (almost the only one of the round, I may add. On the second hole I reverted to type).

The incident, however, provides a clue to one aspect of temperament which is common to most successful players: they are performers in the dramatic sense or, in the crudest terms, show-offs. The most successful ones complement their natural tendency with a touch of showmanship. Arnold Palmer's extrovert personality bubbles more vividly when he is within view of the TV cameras; Doug Sanders takes great pains to 'produce' himself effectively with his extravagant wardrobe. It is good for business, of course, but I suspect it is also good for their golf by satisfying an instinctive appetite and also intimidating more reticent opponents. The same players are uplifted by the galleries and inspired to play above themselves.

Golf is the loneliest of all games, not excluding postal chess. On the course the player is utterly alone, dependant on himself. A thousand spectators may be watching a shot but they can never 'see' it. They observe the external results but the real game is played in the mind of the golfer. He is the only person who knows what is going on.

The roars of 'Good shot!' or groans of sympathy are often irrelevant and wildly inaccurate in their verdict. The quality of a stroke can only be judged in relation to the player's intention. From behind the ropes we cannot judge the problems because they are mainly creations of the player's own mind. That's where the battle is fought and the day is won or lost. What looks like a good shot may be quite different from what the golfer intended and seemingly poor strokes can actually represent considerable victories against powerful forces.

Some of the greatest players carried their loneliness off the course and cultivated it. Henry Cotton and Ben Hogan were players who kept themselves to themselves. By doing so they hardened the competitive edge to their natures. It is easier to do down a stranger than a friend and so, subconsciously—obviously they did not deliberately remain aloof for tactical purposes—they preserved their apartness.

Most golfers, however, react to the loneliness of their work by seeking the warmth of companionship off the course and this makes for a congenial atmosphere in the village of tournament golf. The toughness of their profession demands a hardness of character but this has to be directed inwards as self-discipline. As a result the touring pros are mainly a cheerful lot, generous and excellent company. Of all the different categories of sportsmen I have known there is no group with whom I would rather live and work than the golfers.

Let me now take you round some of the more important sites where the circuses regularly pitch their tents on the annual circuit.

The major championships of world stature are the Open Championship, commonly called the British Open to distinguish it from other national championships, the U.S. Open and the Masters.

The story of the British Open is very largely the story of golf itself, and I have already written about it extensively in the first chapter. It is run by the championship committee of the Royal and Ancient Golf Club and held each July on one of the great seaside links courses.

When the Open began in 1860 it had to be played on links because these were the only courses of championship standard. By the time some of the great inland courses had been built the links tradition was firmly established and there was a strong school of thought which held that seaside golf was the only true form of the game. High winds, hard undulating fairways and glassy greens were considered as virtues to test the mettle of a golfer both as a player and a man. In recent years the conception of golf as primarily a test of skill in which chance should be eliminated as far as possible has gained ground. But the R. and A., no matter how enlightened they may be in this respect, are prisoners of their inherited tradition. Even if they wanted to stage the Open inland, perhaps to bring it to the London area or Manchester, they face two problems. The first of these is that the Open has to be self-supporting and so they must go to areas where financial success, on past evidence, is assured. An unproved venue would involve a considerable risk and failure at the turnstiles could jeopardize the following year's championship.

The second, and more cogent, reason for staying at the seaside is that an Open requires a large area for the tented village, parking and practice grounds and the inland courses of championship standard do not possess this vital amenity. So the seaside has it. Some critics see this as a weakness of the Open since it gives an advantage to the specialists. This argument is not supported by results. For the last fifty years at least the winners have been exclusively men who played most of their golf inland, proving that a great golfer can adapt to any conditions. My own view is that some of the illustrious links on the championship roster are bad golf courses but while this may be heresy it does not deny that the best players come out on top. What I do feel, however, is that the finishing order of say the leading five players may be something of a lottery at times.

The United States Golf Association has much more scope in staging the American Open and they set about the task with all the energy and thoroughness of a big business operation, which indeed is exactly what it is. Every corner of the nation is favoured in time and the list of past Open sites reads like a gazetteer of the United States. (My favourite, incidentally, is the Myopia Hunt Club, Massachussets. I have never been there but every time I see the name it starts a train of thought. What is a Myopia Hunt? It conjures up a picture of short-sighted men in pink coats groping their way across the countryside in blundering and forlorn pursuit of an openly contemptuous fox.)

Well before an Open is played preparations for the next one are in train. The championship committee visit the chosen club and decide how the course shall be prepared. The rough must be allowed to encroach further here . . . that bunker must be enlarged . . . this tee will be moved further back. U.S.G.A. men take up residence at the club for a year to supervise the work and to co-ordinate the administrative plans of the club and Association. All this may sound excessively fussy but all I can say is that the result is magnificent and everything works. If you buy a soft drink from a kiosk on the course you can be sure that there will be a litter-bin at hand for the empty can when you finish it two holes further on. And six holes later there will be a little hut discreetly shielded by the trees. These amenities were not sited by happy accident; some-one you can be sure has researched with slide-rule and flow-chart.

The two Open championships have their own individual flavours. In America you are aware of the efficiency of the operation. Officials, uniformed and labelled, are everywhere, each performing one specific function. It is rather like an enormous clock with a man on every cog and spindle, ready with his oil can. The clock never misses a beat.

The British Open is informal by comparison and everything seems to happen spontaneously. It is difficult to tell who is sup-posed to be doing what. If you really search you discern a few men in tweed jackets and wearing discreet badges with 'Committee' on them. I once saw one of them break into quite a brisk walk but there are very few signs of organizing actually taking place. Yet organization—and very smooth at that—is apparent. Both the British and American methods work and both have an individual charm. I really cannot say which I prefer.

British correspondents who are sent on assignments in a westerly direction, that is to Canada, the Americas or the West Indies, have a special problem. Because of the time difference they frequently have to file reports for their first editions within minutes of touch-ing down.

Your experienced Fleet Street man, on the way to report, say, an uprising in a South American republic, takes this daunting situation in his stride. Once settled on the plane he pulls from his pocket a buff-coloured file marked 'Civil Disorders, South America, 1968—' and stamped prominently 'In NO circumstances may this file be removed from the offices of the *Daily Trumpet*'. From this he can write the background which forms the bulk of his report and only requires to put an up-to-the-minute 'nose' on it. That vital ingredient, by tradition and the exigencies of time, is provided by the taxi driver who drives him from the airport to the cable office. If the driver proves taciturn . . . well, any foreign man worth his place at the bar in El Vino is imaginative and well enough informed to get by. But you see the importance of the taxi driver, fictitious or not. He provides personal involvement, the common touch, an essential whiff of immediacy and a useful entry for expenses.

The cabbie-philosopher is indeed a valued convention although in real life he seems to be a pretty rare bird. I usually cop a pimp or tout for dirty pictures but driving from Bush Field to my first Masters golf tournament at Augusta, Georgia, my man came up trumps.

'These guys don't give a damn about the money, he said. 'What's twenty thousand dollars? Hell, that's just chickenshit. It's the honour and glory they want, that's what it is.'

And so it is. When Bobby Jones and his friend Clifford Roberts invited some of the leading golfers of the day to play in the first tournament on their new course in 1934 they had no idea of the colossus they were spawning. If they'd had any inkling of how it would grow I seriously doubt whether they would have continued with it.

The Augusta National Invitation Tournament, now known simply as The Masters, began as a club championship. Four years earlier Bobby Jones had retired from golf to devote his time to his law practice. From then on, golf was to be an occasional relaxation for him, like any other professional man.

He lived at Atlanta and when a 365-acre tree and shrub nursery came on to the market in nearby Augusta he saw the possibilities of turning it into an attractive golf course. The site had everything one could wish: an undulating area with free-draining soil, meandering streams and a profusion of beautiful trees and shrubs which can perhaps best be described by simply listing the names of the holes: White Pine, Red Dogwood, Flowering Peach, Palm Magnolia, Juniper, Pampas, Yellow Jasmine, Carolina Cherry, Camellia, White Dogwood, Golden Bell, Azalea, Chinese Fir, Fire Thorn, Red Bud, Nandina and Holly.

In his travels Jones had formed some clear ideas of what constituted a good golf hole and he called in a noted golf architect, Dr. Alister MacKenzie, to help put them into practice. Essentially Jones wanted a course which would give pleasure to all golfers, which would test the finest play and reward their skill, and which would call for every type of shot in the golfer's repertory. They created a layout which plays between 6,980 yards and 6,250 yards according to the siting of the tee markers so the course can be set up to suit the scope of the members or expanded to extend the best professionals.

The fairways are wide, covering twice the area of most courses. There is little rough and not very vicious stuff at that, and only about thirty bunkers. If this makes Augusta sound easy it is nothing less than the truth; from the forward tees handicap golfers can expect to clip a few shots off their normal scores.

Why, then, don't the professionals murder it? Well, they can get par figures without much difficulty. But in fair conditions par isn't good enough; it's birdies they're after and this is where the subtleties of Jones and MacKenzie make themselves felt.

Consider the second hole, a par 5 which can be stretched to 555 yards. You drive between an avenue of trees to a fairway which slopes gently upwards to a crest, topped by a massive bunker, at about the length of a decent drive. Beyond the bunker the ground falls away fairly steeply and the fairway dog-legs left. The problem is to decide whether to play short of that fairway bunker, leaving two more shots to the green and hope to get down with a single putt. Conservative players such as Billy Casper would not dream of playing this hole in any other way. Adventurous types such as Arnold Palmer and Tony Jacklin may be tempted to go for the jackpot shot. If you have the strength and courage to fly that bunker, your ball gets the massive bonus of the downslope and you can take a mid-iron for your shot to the green and an almost certain birdie.

The reward is rich, but the dangers are great. Miss the line with that huge drive and the trees on either side virtually assure a six. And the extra effort needed for the drive increases the chances of a wayward shot. I saw Jacklin try for a big one off this tee in the 1968 Masters and he pulled the ball seventy yards off line, deep into the trees. His chance of the title was lost with his ball.

Much the same dilemma occurs at the thirteenth, an acute, left-handed dog leg with trees and a stream on the left. And the stream winds across the fairway just in front of the green. The greater the risk you are prepared to take off the tee the greater the prize. A long drive skirting the disaster area on the left opens the way for, say, a four-iron to the green. But if you play safe, to the right side of the fairway, you almost certainly have to play your second shot short of the stream.

Every hole has its peculiar problems which vary with the position of the flag. And since the Masters tournament committee does not permit the caddies to make the standard early-morning reconnaissance to plot the pin positions, the modern technique of mathematical target golf is not possible. For this one week of the year at least the golfer has to rely on his eye and his instincts.

And here of all courses it is vital to get the answers right. The large and undulating greens are extraordinarily difficult to read; Clive Clark three-putted twelve of them in a practice round and told me incredulously afterwards 'And I wasn't putting badly'. From the edge, three putts are par for the huge greens and so it is critical to get close with the approach shot. Putting entirely dominates the tactics at Augusta. The pin positions dictate the position from which the approach shot is best played and this, in turn, establishes the line and strength of the drive.

MARCH OF THE GLADIATORS

Of all the courses I have seen and played, the Augusta National is by far the one which most compels the golfer to concern himself with putting while pulling his driver from the bag, although my own golf has never approached a standard to involve such fine considerations. In short, Augusta is a wonderful test of the whole golfer, in tactics and technique, and the Masters is a championship which hallmarks its winners for all time. With the itinerant championships it is occasionally possible for a second-rater to have a hot week and win but it takes a genuine master to become Masters' Champion.

This fact alone, the chance of graduating under golf's stiffest examination, would ensure the statue of the Masters. There are, of course, other powerful factors such as the magic of Bobby Jones's name, the superb organization and the glorious Georgian setting.

Above all, the Masters is unique for its continuity. It is held every year during the first full week of April (because the massed azaleas around the colonial clubhouse are at their best) and nothing is allowed to disturb this arrangement. When a member of the committee diffidently pointed out one year that the championship date clashed with Holy Week, Clifford Roberts, the iron custodian of the Masters' tradition, replied icily: 'Then change Easter.'

There are changes from time to time. A group of Augusta members form what is known as the Tournament Improvement Committee and the course has been altered in small ways over the years to keep pace with improvements in equipment.

Perhaps it is decided that a bunker needs resiting to inhibit the long-hitters. The work is carried out during the summer, when the course is closed for four months, and any alterations are the subject of anxious inquiry by the players when they arrive the following spring. The motive behind the changes is not the common passion to modernize for the sake of modernization but rather to preserve the essential character of the original layout. Golf courses are living things, an obvious fact, but one commonly overlooked by club committees, and a diehard attitude of 'touch not a single tree' can utterly defeat its own purpose of preserving a course in its original form.

MARCH OF THE GLADIATORS

The outstanding example is St. Andrews, sacred untouchable St. Andrews, which has been allowed to change in character entirely from a fiery links to a lush meadow. It may look the same but it plays quite differently. Ironically, the blame must lie with the preservationists.

The feeling and spirit of the Masters is carefully maintained and very different it is to the circus atmosphere of most golf tournaments. There is a garden-party air about Augusta. The limited ticket allotment is sold four months in advance and many spectators go straight to one of the permanent stands sited at vantage points around the course and settle down for the day.

A favourite spot is a mound behind the tee of the short twelfth. From here sadists can watch the second shots to the eleventh green plopping into the guardian lake, the tee shot at the twelfth doing likewise into a broad stream, and the drives on the thirteenth rattling into the woods. The galleries here may groan in polite sympathy with the victims but under the veneer of civilized manners they are kin to the Coliseum crowds baying for the blood of the gladiators. How they must have relished the exquisite agony of Dow Finsterwald taking eleven strokes to hole the 155-yard twelfth in 1951.

This section of the course is critical and is popularly known as 'Amen Corner'. The official record book of the tournament recalls two incidents here which have gone into golfing lore and which I would dearly love to have seen.

'During the third round of 1953 Count de Benden found his ball lodged in the bank of the brook in front of the 13th green. (The Count was better known as Johnny de Forest and the subject of one of the games' happier literary felicities. He had the habit of standing motionless at address for an unconsiderable time until, in the words of a newspaper correspondent, "down in de Forest something stirred".) After carefully surveying the situation, Johnny decided, although the stream was rather full, that he could play the ball. Thereupon he stripped off his left shoe and sock and rolled his pants above the knee. Johnny next, very carefully, planted the bare foot on the bank and stepped into the water with his well-shod right foot. The spectators who witnessed this incident will long remember the look of incredulity on the affable Count's face as he realised what he had done.'

'While playing the fourth round in 1954, Al Besselink hit his tee shot into the water on No. 12. Finding that the ball had come to rest on a small sandbar in midstream, Al waded out to the spot and succeeded in playing his ball to the green. Then, following the unconscious dictate of long habit, he carefully smoothed out the indentation he had made, leaving an unblemished sandbar for the next golfer.'

The accumulation of incidents year by year, tragic, amusing or heroic, invests the Masters with a richness which cannot be matched by any other tournament anywhere in the world. But for drama the Masters outdid itself in 1968. There had never been anything like it, not even the sensational record 271 by Jack Nicklaus in 1965 which won him his second title with nine strokes in hand and which prompted Bobby Jones to comment: 'Mr. Nicklaus plays a brand of golf with which I am not familiar'.

The 1968 Masters developed into a two-horse race towards the end of the last round. Roberto de Vicenzo, the Argentinian veteran, was 11 shots under par for the tournament after sixteen holes and a television audience of some forty million people watched enthralled as he rolled in a birdie putt on No. 17 to go 12 under. He then three-putted the last green to go back to 11 under and set the target for his rival, Bob Goalby, who was himself 12 under par with two holes left to play at that stage. He three-putted the seventeenth, which levelled the scores, and although he drove into the trees at No. 18, he got a lucky rebound on to the fairway and made his par four. So they had tied and there was huge excitement, and many forecasts about the outcome, at the prospect of a play-off.

Then the roof fell in. It was announced that de Vicenzo's playing-partner, Tommy Aaron, had inadvertently marked down that birdie three on the seventeenth as a four. And under the rules of golf, which are entirely explicit on this point, a four it had to be since de Vicenzo had signed his card and thereby attested that it was a true record of his round. Goalby was the outright winner after all.

Poor Aaron fled the scene instantly the news was known, taking with him a burden of remorse which was itself punishment out of all proportion to the seriousness of his lapse. In most cases, the marking of a partner's card is almost a formality and any error is detected in the scrutiny by the player before signing the card. But happy-go-lucky de Vicenzo signs his cards with the same carefree air with which he obliges young autograph hunters and although he looked at the figures four times before he added his signature I doubt, at this tense moment which was the crowning-point of his distinguished career, that he saw them.

It was a moment to test the sportsmanship of both players and their public deportment that Sunday afternoon was wholly admirable. De Vicenzo's natural charm never deserted him; he accepted total responsibility and sympathized with Aaron. He could not hide the fact that he was bitterly disappointed but the only hint of criticism into which he would be drawn was at his own stupidity.

Goalby's position was even more difficult. Every expression of condolence for de Vicenzo—and he was the popular hero of the hour—served to reflect on Goalby as a man who had sneaked the title by default. Goalby's golden moment of triumph was tarnished by a feeling that he was, at best, a joint winner. Through no fault of his the victory was being made to look hollow.

That evening he was still unable to enjoy the full elation of his achievement and he admitted to me that he would much rather have played-off and lost than be known as having captured the title on a technicality through a close study of the small print in the rules of golf. The vast volume of words in public print, most of which I thought misguided or hysterical, did not help. Many writers took the position that it was absurd that a birdie, witnessed by an unprecedented number of people, should have to be admitted as a par simply because of a clerical oversight.

The logic of this attitude, superficially attractive though it may be, has a serious flaw. The oversight was committed by the player to whom the duty of checking the card is, and always must be, no less a part of the game than actually playing the shots. He is the only person who knows how many strokes he has taken. The spectator may think he knows. But only the player himself can know if, for example, the ball moved at address and thus cost him a penalty stroke. In my opinion, de Vicenzo's lapse with his addition was equivalent to a similar loss of concentration in, say, playing a bunker shot and leaving the ball in the sand. Or driving an inch out of bounds. Or missing a short putt. Granted that it is dreadfully sad but the sanction in every case is a lost shot. Golf is a game of absolutes and not of what-might-have-been, no matter how we may all delude ourselves with thoughts of moral victories as we part with our half-crowns.

Goalby got his green coat and custody of the Masters trophy, a purely formal custody, I may add, since it is a vast silver replica of the clubhouse which needs a bearer party to lift it and which consequently never leaves the club. And he got the cheque which although, as we have heard, may be chickenshit in the context of modern golf prizes, can normally be multiplied fifty-fold by astute commercial exploitation.

And the Masters did not suffer by all the fuss in the long run. The eventual effect was to quicken public interest the following April. Not that this tournament needs any new stimulus in that direction. For although at Augusta they play things down with no fanfares and beating of drums (and blessedly no advertising on the course to disfigure the scene) the more they suppress the commercialism of big sports promotion the more of a novelty the Masters becomes. And, ironically, this policy of making every aspect of the tournament subservient to the ideal that the game is the thing brings them greater commercial success every year.

There is a clear moral here for sponsors. Gimmicky prizes for holes in one and huge fortunes for the winner are not the vital factors to ensure success for a tournament. Great golfers playing a great course are the essentials.

Although golf is a truly international game in that it is played in almost every country in the world, for most nations it is a minority sport enjoyed mainly by the well-to-do. When the late Tony Lema played an exhibition match in Copenhagen the hospitable Danes hired spectators at £5 a head in order that the American star should not feel slighted at playing for a much smaller audience than usual. Much the same sort of thing happened in Rome for a television match. On that occasion the purpose was to make a film for transmission in America and it was necessary that there should not only be a decent sized crowd but that it should react in an orderly and knowledgeable fashion. Film extras were hired from Cine Città, the Hollywood of Italy, and they were rehearsed and directed just as if they were playing crowd scenes for a regular film. Boards were held up instructing them when to clap and to 'Ooh' and to 'Aah'. Being professional actors the result was no less convincing than if a shipload of the burgesses had been imported from St. Andrews.

What the TV audience did not hear, however, was a whispered conversation between two of the extras as they stood behind the eighteenth green. 'At last I'm just beginning to get the hang of what this game is all about,' said one. 'They are having a race to see who can get his ball into the hole first.' 'Exactly,' said his friend, 'but why don't they get a move on?' These two incidents perhaps explain more clearly than statistics the state of public opinion about the game outside the main golfing nations, why golf has not yet found its way into the Olympic games and why international golf events are regarded in many places as curiosities.

For this reason I regard the World Cup competition as the most important event in the international calendar. From a purely golfing point of view it does not yet rate anywhere near as highly as its grand title suggests. For all that, its missionary value is enormous. The man in the street of Rome or Singapore or Mexico City may have only the haziest idea of what the game is all about. But he is immediately intrigued when he learns that the leading players earn as much, and sometimes more, for knocking a ball into a hole in the ground as his own national sporting heroes can get for killing a bull or filling a football stadium. 'There must be something in it' is the reaction. They come, they see and they are enraptured. Wherever the World Cup is played, it generates an enthusiasm for the game which is followed by a surge of recruits and new courses. The World Cup was the idea of an American industrialist, the late John Jay Hopkins, who had the idealistic notion that the rules of golf might prove stronger than the New Testament in fostering international friendship. The validity of this conception seems to be, at the highest valuation, unproven. On the whole the evidence suggests that the overall effect of much international sport is to polarize partisan passions and cause bad blood. Be that as it may, Hopkins formed the International Golf Association with the motto 'International goodwill through golf' and the first tournament was played in Montreal in 1953. In those days the trophy was called the Canada Cup and seven teams competed—Canada, America, Argentina, Australia, Germany, Mexico and a hybrid pairing from South Africa and Great Britain. The Argentinians, Antonio Cerda and the evergreen Roberto de Vicenzo, won the cup and the much-fancied American team of Julius Boros and Jim Turnesa finished well down the field. Since then the United States has, quite naturally, had its share of success, winning the Cup nine times in sixteen attempts.

From its modest beginnings the World Cup has grown each year in prestige. The proud boast of the organizers that it has visited six continents may be one more continent than conservative geographers recognize, but the value of its evangelistic power cannot be denied. It is a splendid occasion with the flags of all the participating nations flying side by side and the golfers swearing at their uncomprehending caddies in a Babel of tongues. Each pairing plays four rounds of medal golf and there is also a trophy for the lowest individual score. The one danger we should guard against is taking the result too seriously, for whatever the World Cup may do it does not produce a valid league table of national golfing merit. And the individual winner is not automatically the world champion. The competition is nothing like comprehensive enough for conclusions of that nature.

Every player wins in the World Cup for apart from the prestige (and resulting cash) value of being chosen to represent his country, he gets his travel and hotel expenses and a useful chunk of appearance money. This makes it an expensive operation to mount and the commercial sponsors get very little return in publicity for their generosity. Their support is patronage rather than sponsorship in the usual sense and for this reason the future of the World Cup cannot be regarded as being so secure as some other commercially-sound golfing enterprises. We must keep our fingers crossed; the ideal of international goodwill through golf deserves that much of us at least.

In America the championship of the United States Professional Golfers' Association is highly esteemed but this, I feel, is more because of what the winner gets out of it than because of particular merit of the event. The P.G.A. champion is invited to play in the World Series, organized by a television company, with the winners of the two Opens and the Masters. Somebody has to make a fourth to be sure and there is not another obvious candidate, but the P.G.A. is hardly to be considered as ranking with the other three.

Two more tournaments (not championships, please) with global pretensions are the Piccadilly World Match-Play event and the Alcan Golfer of the Year. The Piccadilly is played at Wentworth and comprises a field of eight, some of whom are present as of right—U.S. and British Open champions, Masters champion, British Match-Play champion—and some by invitation of the sponsors. By selecting their field in this way the sponsors are able to include great players who are not necessarily current champions and thus they are assured of success, if only for reasons of sentiment. But by reserving places for invitees they have to forfeit the conception of eight leading champions meeting in an end-of-season decider for the topmost of the top dogs.

It is a pity, for the idea of a true world championship of champions is an attractive one. The problems of staging such an event are, however, enormous and the prize fund would have to be vast to ensure full attendance. As it is, the Piccadilly is one of the highlights of the golfing year. Match-play golf has gone out of favour—the pros don't care for it and its too chancy for the static requirements of television—and this is a rare chance to watch the most exciting form of golf. Some of my most vivid memories are of matches in the Piccadilly—Gary Player pulling back a seven-hole deficit to beat Tony Lema, Neil Coles matching Arnold Palmer shot for shot and just being beaten by fortune smiling more bountifully on his opponent. Player again and Tony Jacklin deadlocked after eighteen holes with dusk forcing them to postpone the outcome overnight. After the man-to-man appeal of match play, the usual tournament round of seventy-two holes medal seems sterile indeed.

The Alcan is a truly international tournament or, rather, a series of tournaments. The sponsors designate a number of tournaments on the different world circuits as qualifying events. Each part of the world thus qualifies a certain number of finalists who play off over seventy-two holes. The final is normally held in Britain although it can go to America on occasion, as for instance in 1969. The golfing concept of the Alcan is that it is a comprehensive test, lasting several months and involving a variety of courses and conditions and although the qualifying system is rather complicated it works well enough and the winner has the double satisfaction of knowing that he has played consistently throughout the season—plus the largest prize-cheque golf has to offer.

If these are the plums, the bread-and-butter pudding of the tournament circuits is made up of events sponsored by firms, localities or individuals. There has been a dramatic expansion of tournament golf since the War and more changes are certainly on the way. The British circuit must surely amalgamate with Europe and eventually I believe there must be a rationalization of dates and events. When that day comes there will be a graduated system of tournament golf. At the lowest level there will be a calendar of national events, C circuits if you like, on which young pros will cut their competitive teeth.

The B grade will be five continental circuits and the heavy mob of superstars will form the A grade who will travel the world playing only in the big money, big prestige events. There is a long way to go before this comes about—the level of prize funds would have to increase tenfold in some cases to tempt the American pros away from home for long stretches—but golf is slowly and inevitably moving in that direction. I only hope I live to see it.

4

Golf is people

JOURNALISTS, as everyone knows, are hard-bitten and cynical. The laws of libel and the conventions of decency prevent them from writing all they know about celebrities. But the undished dirt is common knowledge among the expense account fraternity; hero-worship has no place in the press clubs. That, at least, is the reputation of Fleet Street, actively fostered in some quarters and not entirely undeserved. It is probably nearer the truth to classify newspaper men with valets in this context and say that only really exceptional men can remain heroes to the writers.

In the case of golf correspondents the giants of the sport are at a particular disadvantage. The routine at most tournaments is that players who have done particularly well or particularly badly are led into the press tent for interview after their newsworthy round. So golfers are exposed at both extremes of the emotional spectrum—during the elation of a course record or the despair of a disaster, both moments when a man will reveal unsuspected sides of his true nature no matter how hard he tries to guard his 'image'.

Jack Nicklaus is a good example. Being such a big name he is 'news' whatever he does and is an automatic visitor to the press tent after every round. His moods reflect his score, of course, but during a tournament he is always inclined to be edgy, quick with a cutting reply for the fatuous question (of which there are many, some deliberate for the daft question has its place in a skilled interview technique) and generally impatient. At the end of the tournament, however, especially if it is one which he has narrowly lost, the real Jack Nicklaus stands up. Win or lose he is relaxed, expansive and generous about his fellow competitors. While others hurry away to douse the fires of disappointment under the shower or drive their fists into locker-room doors, Nicklaus is content to sit sipping a soft drink and talk reflectively about the day's events. A notable occasion was when one incautious shot—an out-of-bounds drive—cost him the 1968 Open Championship at Carnoustie. By the time he finished the round every trace of self-recrimination had vanished. In the tent he was philosophic about it all and when the coversation was led into a discussion of golfing techniques and course architecture, he gave a discourse which was highly rewarding to the serious student of the game.

But this is not making my point about hero worship. For although I consider Nicklaus to be the finest living golfer when he is at the top of his form, Arnold Palmer is the man I had in mind when I said that no man, supposedly, is a hero to the reporter.

At the Schweppes' tournament in Hunstanton in 1967 we gathered for a drink and a chat and the talk was about golf and golfers. It nearly always is on these occasions; British golf correspondents are obsessional in their enthusiasm. One of the party, an experienced Fleet Street-man whose capacity for enthusiasm had been jaded by a lifetime of recording human follies, had monopolized the conversation with a running eulogy of Palmer, laced with telling anecdotes to illustrate the qualities of the great man. Even among golf correspondents there comes a point where enough is enough. One rash spirit interrupted the flow of Palmer-worshipping hyperbole with a gentle demur. Of course Palmer was great but surely it was a disservice to him to lay it on too thick. The monologue now became a heated discussion:

'Arnold Palmer is the greatest human being who ever lived.'

'What about Jesus Christ?'

'Palmer is greater than Christ!'

'Could Palmer have walked on the water then?'

'No need. Arnie would have *carried* the water.'

This ridiculous exchange shows the measure of how deep an impact Palmer has made on some, admittedly extreme, elements in the sporting public. He promotes fanaticism. Wherever golf is played there are volunteers for Arnie's Army who would willingly impose their heads into the path of an overhit shot from their hero in order that the ball might rebound on to the green. Bruises so won are medals to be proudly worn as proof of loyalty under fire. The blasphemous Palmerphile above maintains a shrine to him in his home, complete with sacred relics and a driver which was once used by the saint.

The atmosphere in Arnie's Army is infectious and I was myself once momentarily touched by the spell. It was at Wentworth during the memorable final of the Piccadilly match-play tournament between Palmer and Neil Coles. At the twelfth hole I had abandoned all hope of infiltrating the crush around the tee to watch the drives and had walked forward to station myself at a good vantage point for the second shots. I guessed well. Palmer pulled his drive and his ball came to rest within a yard of where I stood by the ropes, partially stymied by a tree. As he weighed up the shot and tested his backswing, the Army came crashing through the undergrowth and formed up in a tight, compassionate press behind me. Palmer decided to chip back to the centre of the fairway and took his stance. At that moment a female trooper somehow insinuated herself in front of me, placed the spiked point of her shooting-stick on my right foot and sat down. Neither by sound or twitching muscle did I betray the excruciating agony until Palmer had completed his stroke. I can think of no other player who would induce me to stand still for that sort of treatment.

It is not difficult to see why Palmer inspires his followers. Where other players are aloof and hide their feelings under an impassive mask, Palmer is all too obviously human. He suffers and the crowd suffers with him. They share his obvious joy. And when he gets himself into trouble—not infrequently with his dashing game—if there is half a chance of a dramatic recovery he will go for it. The narrowest gap in the trees is all he needs to persuade him to have a go. His gambler's instinct finds a natural response in the gallery. And there is no more exciting spectacle in golf than watching Palmer stake everything on one bold shot. The Palmer legend is based on upsetting the odds; either by retrieving seemingly hopeless situations with a dashing 'charge' or rashly dissipating a commanding lead. Both results are exciting and endearing.

By themselves, Palmer's personality and skill would have made him into a successful tournament player and brought him a comfortable living and due honours. But no more, I daresay, than any of his equally gifted contemporaries. What made him into an international institution, the wealthiest and best known sportsman of all time and the instrument of a revolution which changed golf all over the world was the partnership which began with a casual conversation early in his professional career.

Mark McCormack, a young lawyer of driving ambition and energy who had first noticed Palmer when they played in opposing college golf teams, had formed an organization to arrange exhibition matches for professionals. Palmer was a client and one day he asked McCormack if he would be interested in handling all his affairs. McCormack agreed. The arrangement was that he should take over all the tedious administrative details of bookings, contracts and schedules and leave Palmer free to devote all his attention to playing golf.

It was by no means the first time that a golfer had teamed up with a manager, or agent. The significance of this partnership was that it started at a time when the social and economic climate was favourable for an expansion of golf and here was a man with the ability to exploit his client's success presented with the hottest, most exploitable property in sport. It is sometimes asked whether Palmer made McCormack or McCormack made Palmer. The question, it seems to me, misses the point. They both did their jobs supremely well, thanks to each other. Because of McCormack, Palmer was able to win the Masters four times, the British Open twice, the U.S. Open, become the leading money-winner of all time and the unofficial world champion. With that sort of ammunition in his gun McCormack was able to storm the smoke-filled rooms and dictate terms to the men who controlled the money. They were happy to pay up. Both McCormack and Palmer became millionaires in the process but that

is a private irrelevance. For the public the side effects of the partnership were enormous. The fame of Palmer pulled in the fans, both
to the course and into the TV audience, and having watched they
wanted to play. Golf in America exploded in the wake of Palmer's
progress.

He travelled the world. Palmer has a genuine element of missionary zeal in his personality; McCormack turned Palmer's travels
to shrewd advantage. Palmer played in the British Open and re-
vitalized it in the process, restoring its faded prestige as the premier
championship. Wherever he played Palmer provided the catalyst for
surge in golfing interest. It is always difficult to place the achievements of one man in historical perspective while he is still around,
but I am confident that Palmer's influence as a popularizer of the
game will come to be seen as a contribution more significant than
the impact of Harry Vardon and Bobby Jones. They were possibly
greater players but they were minority heroes. In their days golf was
limited to a few by the expense of it. But, above all, they did not
have McCormacks behind them.

The contribution of McCormack is no less obvious. His association with Palmer was followed by similar arrangements with Gary
Player, Jack Nicklaus and a string of other slightly less illustrious
players including Tony Jacklin, Peter Townsend, Clive Clark and
Peter Oosterhuis of Britain, Bobby Cole the brilliant South African
and Bob Charles, the left-hander from New Zealand. McCormack's
interests spread into other sports and spheres and his clients later
included tennis players, football stars, ski champions and a song
writer.

McCormack is shy of words like empire and is sensitive to suggestions that his power gave him enough influence to manipulate the
sports with which he was associated. Most such accusations, on
investigation, are seen to spring from jealousy and are without substance. Of course he has a decisive finger in many golfing pies. And
I have no doubt that in some instances his influence is not always
entirely beneficial for golf. But against that he can reflect that his
activities on behalf of his clients have raised the status of the game

enormously. He put golf in the big time. Because of him, prize money has escalated, contract rates have improved and the standard of living of the professional golfer has, at a conservative estimate, doubled. He is seldom given credit for these achievements on the grounds that while they may be true enough they were accidental side effects of his personal ambitions. Such a view seems to me to be uncharitable, on a par with denying Napoleon the credit for unifying Europe because of selfish personal ambitions. On the balance sheet of golf McCormack must be entered as a substantial asset.

My elevation of Palmer above Bobby Jones may seem surprising since the evidence in support of Jones as the greatest golfer of all time is strong and, to my mind, decisive. Perhaps I had better make this point absolutely clear. I see Palmer as the most *important* golfer of modern times, Jones as the *best* player of this or any other age.

Robert Tyre Jones Junior was one of those tiresome creatures, a boy prodigy. Of all youthful traits, precocity is the most powerful irritant so far as I am concerned and if a replica of the young Jones were to come upon the golf scene these days, I am sure I should be tempted to kick him. The very idea of a six-year-old in velvet shorts playing a violin with the virtuosity of a master repels me. (I may say that I admire Mr. Yehudi Menuhin enormously now.) It utterly devalues the virtue of years of practice and honest application and is a humiliating reproach to honest plodders, or so it seems to honest plodding me. Dammit, it's *unfair*! And in the case of young Jones the itching toe in boot would be intensified by the fact that the brattish youth had a deplorable temper to match his reddish hair. He threw clubs about and swore and tore up his card and behaved generally in a manner which moves middle-aged squares like me to suggest that what that young man needs is a stint in the army to give him a wholesome touch of discipline.

Fortunately for the teenager from Atlanta, his talent did not lie in a field in which temperament is considered a virtue. Had he been a musician or an actor he must surely have developed into one of the outstanding four-letter men of all time. Golf, however, is a stern disciplinarian. Angry men simply cannot play it well, they must

either learn to control their emotions or be content to play badly—
or give up the game altogether. (The only exception to this rule I
ever heard of was a choleric character who solved the problem of an
explosive temper by playing without a ball. He swings, judges where
the ball would have gone and plays to a steady scratch standard
quite happily.)

In time golf mellowed Jones. He learnt how to channel his powerful personality into a positive ally on the course and this, for him,
was the hardest task of his golfing apprenticeship. The business of
swinging a club came easily to him, under the gruff and forthright
tutelage of Stewart Maiden, the Scottish pro at Atlanta, and his own
intelligent experimenting.

During the time of Jones's career—1927 to 1935—the disparity
between the best amateur golf and professional standards was hardly
to be considered and the four major titles were the British and U.S.
Open and Amateur championships. Jones, the son of a lawyer, was
an amateur, of course, and as he took the golf world by storm people
began to speculate on the possibility, so remote as to be hardly within
human compass, that he might win all four championships in one
year. They called it the Grand Slam and it is difficult to explain to
non-golfers exactly what such a task entailed. In cricketing terms it
might be compared to a batsman scoring a century in each of the
ten innings of a Test series; or a ten-pin bowler playing all night
without once leaving a skittle standing. Theoretically possible for an
outstanding player but very, very improbable.

In 1930 Jones achieved his Grand Slam. In his eight playing years
he won thirteen national championships (having played in only
twenty-one) and dominated the game to the extent that for the most
part the others were virtually playing for second place. As Charley
Price, editor of his instructional book (*Bobby Jones on Golf*, Cassell),
put it: 'No amateur or professional golfer before or since Jones has
come close to compiling such a record, and nobody with any sense
could imagine that anybody else ever will.'

In fact the target is no longer there to be shot at. These days the
amateur championships cannot begin to be classified among the

world's leading events. A Grand Slam today would have to take in the U.S. and British Opens, the Masters and possibly, although arguably and a poor fourth, the American P.G.A. Championship. The chances of one man winning those in the same year are so slim that the Grand Slam is no longer a subject for intelligent discussion.

The fact of Jones's victories is less remarkable than the manner in which he won them. Anyone less like the dedicated golfers of today, men who play and practice for up to eight hours a day six days a week, would be hard to imagine. Jones was not only an amateur but he was a part-timer in the sense suggested by the Italian designation: *dilletante*. Golf accounted for a surprisingly small proportion of his time. Sometimes he went for three months at a time without touching a club and his preparation for a championship would often be no more than a practice round or two. He had other things to occupy his attention. During those eight years when he was casually turning the world of golf on its ear he also took his law degree, another degree in mechanical engineering and a third in English Literature, at Harvard University. From these accomplishments it may be deduced, and rightly so, that Jones was a man of catholic interests and exceptional intellectual capacity.

For the new generations of golfers the playing record of Bobby Jones has probably receded into dusty regions of history. There are more enduring legacies for today's players. In his travels he played many golf courses and formed firm opinions about the qualities which were required in a golf hole for a fair but demanding test of golf. (Like many others before him his first impression of the Old Course at St. Andrews was far from favourable but over the years he came to respect its subtleties.) His accummulated ideas about golf-course architecture eventually found brilliant expression in the Augusta National course, the home of the Masters.

Jones was a serious student of golf techniques and here he was helped by his academic background. The engineer in him made his approach to the golf swing both analytical and practical; the literary side of his interests gave him the sensitivity and the words to express his thoughts in vivid, readable prose. His description of the shaft of a golf club, for instance, as an imponderable connecting the hands and clubhead is an acute, scientific assessment of the shaft's function (contrary to the clap-trap with which club manufacturers still try to bamboozle the gullible public) as well as a graphic expression of what the player should feel. Jones was a prolific writer and the book I mentioned earlier is a collection of his newspaper articles. One of his aphorisms was 'Nobody ever swung a golf club too slowly'. Of his writing I am tempted to say 'Nobody ever read Jones too thoroughly'.

At the age of twenty-eight, at the height of his golfing career, Jones retired from the scene. He had achieved every playing ambition and his competitive edge was subconsciously slightly blunted. His law practice and other interests were calling. And although he has never admitted such an immodest thought, I am sure that he realized the danger that if he continued to monopolize the titles, the monotony of it might have a stultifying effect on the game.

Although golf lost its most gifted player his influence on the game continued in rich measure. His teaching, as a writer and film-maker, stimulated interest and raised playing standards and the growing scope of his own tournament, the Masters, set a new yardstick against which golfers might measure their stature.

Two South Africans have profoundly influenced the post-war development of golf. The first time I saw Bobby Locke on the course I experienced something of the awe that one feels on watching a stage illusionist. I had heard about his famous 'draw', of course, how he hit every shot so that it moved from right to left in the air and I had read about his uncanny putting skill and his expressionless appearance. However none of the written descriptions prepared me for the reality.

By that time Locke was nearing the end of a remarkable career; he was a venerable figure in golf lore and fitted the part. For a start, he did not look like a golfer. He was portly, and walked slowly with that noble belly distended like the mainsail of a man-o-war running free before the wind. In his plus-fours and white cap he seemed out of place on a golf course—as if some noble figure, say the Lord Chief Justice, had been kidnapped by hooligans, dressed in fancy clothes and been forced to run the gauntlet of the vulgar throng. This impression was strengthened by the demeanour of the man. He walked slowly up the centre of the fairway, alone with his dignity, and looking neither to right nor left. Upon reaching the ball he looked at it distastefully and selected a club from the bag proffered by a respectful attendant. A real golfer at this point paces up and down measuring distances from the nearest marker, tosses a pinch of grass into the air to test the breeze, consults the caddie about the state of the green, has at least two full rehearsals of the swing, and then spends upwards of a minute shuffling and waggling himself into the correct position and state of mind.

Locke took the club, swung it idly once with the air of a man who'd never seen one before and wasn't impressed now that he had, stepped up to the address and, with the casual action of brushing a crumb from a tablecloth, struck the ball towards the trees on the right of the fairway. Without pausing to watch the flight of the shot, he handed the club back to his caddie and resumed his stately progress straight towards the green.

The ball, seeming mindful all of a sudden of its impertinence at flying towards the out-of-bounds after being struck by the great man, now applied sharp left rudder and came slanting back towards the target and landed with a repentant plop by the flagstick.

On the green Locke's look of disdain for the futility of the exercise appeared stronger than ever. He looked briefly at the line of the putt and took out a putter so old and rusty that no self-respecting golfer would dare be seen handling it. Locke then stood by the ball and with the air of someone who has lost the instructions for a do-it-yourself kit and has got to work it out for himself, tried two experimental swings. Satisfied that this must be how the implement was designed to be used, he moved forward and struck the putt smoothly into the hole. Sometimes he missed them. Either way, the spectator could get no clue from Locke's expression about what he was feeling. It seemed that he felt nothing at all.

Locke's mask of impassivity was, of course, just that—a mask. As a young man Locke learned three lessons and he applied them more thoroughly than any of his contemporaries. The first was to control his emotions. Every golfer knows that once you have hit a bad shot there is nothing you can do about it but it takes a large effort of will to translate this knowledge into practical effect. Locke deliberately cultivated a slow, measured routine so that he would have time to eliminate all traces of anger and disappointment from his system and set his mind to the positive thought of playing the next shot well.

Having mastered his emotions Locke learnt how to conceal them. He has written how he began to notice the nervous reactions of his opponents—how his rival in the final of the Transvaal Amateur Championship, four up and six to play, reacted to Locke's holing of a long putt by turning pale, walking faster to the next tee and hitting a poor drive. He realized his opponent was shaken and this knowledge inspired him to go on and win at the nineteenth.

Until he noticed those tell-tale signs Locke had thought the match was virtually lost and he realized that if he could benefit from knowing how opponents were feeling, they could likewise do the same with him. He determined that he would never show any inner turbulence by as much as an unconscious twitching of a muscle. Of course he felt emotions; the golfer has not been born who is impervious to the tensions of tournament play and Locke on occasions felt physically sick at missing important putts. But he was the only person who knew about it. I doubt if any player before or since has gone on to a golf course with thicker psychological armour. He seemed unflappable and therefore invincible.

The third element of Locke's golfing philosophy was that just as he gave nothing away to his opponents and capitalized on their reactions, so he allowed nothing of their play to affect him. He played the course, going for the pars, and that left the others fighting him.

Cocooned in an envelope of tranquillity, the fireproof man was a match for anyone. Sam Snead in his prime could win only twice in a sixteen-match challenge series against Locke. The South African won four Open Championships and on his American raids—where he slept with his beloved putter for fear of losing it—he plundered the rich prize funds until the home pros, who had scoffed at 'Old Muffin Face', squealed in frustration. These are fair compensations to set against the unjust reputation of being cold and aloof.

South Africa's second major figure in world golf is, of course, Gary Player and in many ways he is the opposite of Locke. No one is ever in any doubt about Player's innermost feelings and his quick and articulate tongue dispels any possibility of ambiguity. Where Locke turned all emotions inwards, Player blazes forth. His outspoken comments about deficiences in the preparation of courses, spectator behaviour, caddies or any other golfing subject are as much part of the Player legend as his capacity for rising to the big occasion. A few well-publicized incidents, such as the occasion in the Piccadilly semi-final against Tony Jacklin when he upbraided the gallery for what he thought to be undue partiality, has earned him the reputation of being something of a fire-brand. The pity of it is that in some quarters these outbursts are given undue importance and cloud a proper appreciation of his genius as a golfer. In some ways he is the most remarkable golfer of our time. For Player is the supreme example of the seven-stone weakling who returned to kick sand into the face of the beach bully.

He is short, five foot seven, and was slightly built as a youth. And so although he showed an immediate aptitude when he began golf he was neither big enough nor strong enough to hit the ball far. What he lacked in physique he made up for in zeal. Most small people are driven to 'show them', to make up for their size by excelling in some way and many of the world's major disasters can be laid at the size-seven feet of little men trying to prove they are big.

In Player's case the complex took an unusual direction. Instead of becoming excessively cunning, or clever, or influential, his ambition took the form of becoming a superman. And he succeeded. His fanaticism, abetted by a religious fervour which at times revealed to him his destiny in letters of fire, drove him to a punishing physical régime.

He practised for longer hours than anyone. He ran to build up his legs, and he did finger-tip pressups to develop the hands and arms. He pushed himself to what felt like the limit of human endurance and then proved it wasn't by continuing his exercises. And when he broke through into big-time golf and found that he was still conceding an advantage to players like Palmer and Nicklaus, who could hit the par-five holes in two shots, he redoubled his muscle-building efforts. He became a food-and-health faddist. And, although genuinely religious, it is possible also fair to say that the main temple of worship was his own body. And he had his reward. The hours of weight-training and exercises, not to mention the nuts and honey, paid off. He did hit the ball as far as all but the outstandingly long-players. And since the distance which a ball can be hit depends largely on the length of the golfer's arms (about which Player could do nothing, doubtless to his disappointment) the fact that he was the equal off the tee meant that he was hitting harder than the others.

In other words, as I have remarked before, in order to play as well as Nicklaus he had to play better than Nicklaus. In order to hit the ball as far as Palmer he had to hit it more powerfully than Palmer. His 156 pounds had to produce more strength than his rivals' 200 pounds.

Player's classic record of U.S. Open, P.G.A. Championship, Masters and two British Opens compares favourably with that of any other golfer. When he took those titles he was demonstrably the best player in the world. Although it is possible to over-emphasize the importance of physical stature in golf, Player's feats can surely be compared with that of a middleweight winning the heavyweight championship.

His story, as he reminds us—rather too often for some tastes—is a triumph for dedication and hard work. I sometimes wonder whether the world would ever have heard of Gary Player if he had been a six-footer. Somehow I think it unlikely.

In this chapter on golf personalities I have limited myself to latter-day players who, in my opinion, have made major contributions to the arts of the game—Palmer's showmanship, Jones's skill,

Locke's psychology, Player's dedication. It is an arbitrary distinction and a pity, for it means that many wonderful and colourful characters must be omitted. But a line must be drawn somewhere and if many outstanding practitioners such as Ben Hogan, Byron Nelson, Henry Cotton, Billy Casper, Dai Rees and Max Faulkner, are dismissed with a respectful nod, it should not be taken as an expression of opinion as to their standing as golfing heroes.

But in any review which attempts to analyse the dominant factors which have brought great players to the fore, a place must be found for Peter Thomson who has won five Open championships, only one fewer than Harry Vardon's record, and who is acknowledged even by his detractors as the finest player of the small ball of his era.

Thomson is in the Bobby Locke tradition in that he manages to conceal his emotions on the course and the main distinction which I would draw between them is that whereas Locke appeared dour and unbending, the Australian gives the impression of enjoying a private joke. Even at the tensest moments he wears a serene Mona Lisa-smile which thoroughly belies his newspaper soubriquet of 'the Melbourne Tiger'. If Thomson is to be likened to a tiger it must be one which has just consumed a particularly plump canary. Like Locke, however, it is a public face and hides a resolute will and an emotional turmoil. But the key to his enormous success lies, I feel, in his intellect. No one would rate him an outstanding striker of the ball for although he is technically faultless, he never uses his full power. Most of his opponents out-drive him, often by considerable distances.

This does not worry Thomson; as far as he is concerned it is totally irrelevant. His method is to analyse a golf course with the precision of an engineer surveying the route for a road. He mentally works out angles and distances and prepares contingency plans for different weather conditions.

During the 1968 Open Championship at Carnoustie he and Billy Casper, another highly intelligent golfer, spent over half an hour discussing the tactics for playing what seemed to me to be a perfectly straightforward two-shot hole. Thomson knows exactly where he wants to place the ball on every shot. All players to some extent play 'percentage golf'; that is, they weigh possible advantages against potential dangers and reach a compromise according to their temperaments, the bold ones taking chances, and the timorous playing safe. Generally this is a haphazard process of glancing down the fairway and deciding 'better keep it over to the right to avoid that bunker' then repeating the treatment on the next shot. The vast majority of golfers use this system, or lack of system, of taking each shot as it comes. In Thomson's case the procedure is reversed. He plans backwards, first deciding where he wants to hit the green and then choosing a point from which this objective would best be achieved. That, in turn, governs the tactics for his drive. Throughout all this planning he is balancing the ideal situation against the margin of error, which he knows all too well, in his own performance.

With all this I would be quite wrong if I gave the impression that in play Thomson is an automaton responding to mathematical programming. He is perhaps the last of the 'instinctive' players and is full of scorn for the new generation of golfers who have to use elaborate diagrams and pace off every shot, even a flick with a wedge, against a pre-measured marker. For although his strategy is rational he relies entirely on his eye, his judgement and that educated 'feel' which sometimes prompts an experienced golfer to hit an easy four wood where, on a strictly mathematical basis, he could very well take a three iron. That is how golf ought to be played, he feels, and he once suggested to me that it would be instructive to hold a tournament on a course which none of the competitors had been allowed to see before they teed up for the first round. No yardage marked on the tees or cards, no caddies allowed to pace the course, no distance markers.

Thomson is rather given to this type of impishly pointed suggestion; he knows better than anyone that if such a tournament could be arranged, with the players coming to it 'cold', there could only be one winner: Peter Thomson of Australia.

For all that—and he loses no chance to twist the tails of the American superstars for whom he has no great love (an attitude which it must be admitted is mutual)—Thomson has a genuine feeling for the traditions of golf. He loves the Old Course at St. Andrews and is appalled to see its fiery character mellowed by the new automatic-sprinklers and fairway-fertilizers.

These days Thomson limits his tournament appearances as the calls of his other interests, golf-course architecture and the administration of the game in Australasia, makes increasing demands on his time. However it is gratifying that in these days when so many architects are obsessed by length, vying with each other to produce monsters, there are some new courses being built by a man who believes that golf is a game which should involve brain as much as brawn in which subtleties are paramount.

In the opposite corner to Thomson is Jack Nicklaus who sees golf less as an art than as an exact science. The immensely powerful American was not the first man to pace-off golf courses and make personal maps with short notes about distances and the quality of the rough—but he developed it into a golfing credo. He has been accused of being a cold fish (and a great many other and worse things than that. His treatment by a section of the golf-watching public when he first began toppling their idol, Palmer, was one of the nastiest manifestations I have known in golf).

For Nicklaus the accusations about lack of feeling are entirely pointless. To him a golf shot is a problem of mechanics. After one round of the 1967 Open Championship he was in the interview tent and someone asked him about a spoon shot he had played into the teeth of a stiff wind and which his caddie had boasted travelled 286 yards. Was this, Nicklaus was asked with awe, a correct measurement? Most players would have replied with a self-satisfied mock modesty along the lines of 'Well, I guessed I nudged it along pretty good.'

Nicklaus reacted with the testy air of an accountant who has discovered an error in the petty cash. 'When I struck the ball I was 261 yards from the hole. It finished 40 feet short. So the ball travelled 248 yards.' When the next questioner asked him if he took notice of how other competitors were faring he answered 'Oh yes.

I'm human.' At that moment the reassurance seemed almost necessary.

Golf for Nicklaus means measuring exact distances, correcting for wind and any other special factors such as exceptionally hard conditions, selecting the appropriate club and executing the shot. And when he is on top of his form, and putting well, he is in a class by himself. The others might as well go home. Because of his approach he takes immense pains in setting up for a shot, making minute adjustments in the alignments of his feet and the clubhead before committing himself to the swing. No man since Hogan has come so close to turning himself into a perfect golfing machine.

It is as well for golf that neither of them has achieved their goal. In practice for the U.S. Open in 1967 Nicklaus had a remarkable round over the tough Baltusrol course—from memory it was a 63— and afterwards he was asked how many strokes he felt had been completely satisfactory. 'Not one, but the score was.'

For the spectator Nicklaus has always seemed to me to be the most exciting player of them all. With most professionals the handicap player can identify himself since the shots he sees are within his own capability, however rare or remote the possibility. In Nicklaus's case this situation does not apply. When he really exerts himself he hits the ball in a manner totally outside normal human experience. And if he can be persuaded to indulge in a little exhibition stuff— strictly off duty and well away from a tournament; he is far too serious minded for such frivolities when there is work to be done —he can perform feats of strength which you would not believe possible.

Most golfers indulge in harmless flights of fancy from time to time, such as winning the Open, but my favourite Walter Mitty pastime is to caddie for Nicklaus round my own course with the added privilege (this is a daydream and no condition is too fanciful) that he did exactly what I told him, without arguments. 'Take a line on that hummock and give it *everything*.' 'Never mind those trees, really belt that ball with just a suspicion of fade!' I wonder what it would cost to hire him for half a day....

F

Strictly speaking, Tony Jacklin has not achieved the stature of Palmer, Player and Nicklaus at the time at which I am writing but his more modest successes make him a significant figure simply because of his nationality.

Since the end of the Second World War British professional golf has played a muted second fiddle to the American game and British professionals, with the exception of Max Faulkner's Open Championship of 1951, have walked in the shadows of the transatlantic superstars.

Confidence is the absolute essence of good golf and in the young self-confidence is apt to show itself as a cocky brashness. The virtues which he displays today as a golfer could be seen as faults in the young Jacklin. He was self-willed and cocky and impatient with his elders to the point of impertinence.

Jacklin's father, a lorry driver, wanted him to learn a steady trade and become a respectable skilled worker in a Scunthorpe factory. Jacklin was determined to become a golfer. He defied his parents and had the immense good fortune, although he did not appreciate it at the time, to be taken on as an assistant to Bill Shankland at Potters Bar.

Shankland, a tough and uncompromising Australian, recognized that young Jacklin possessed championship qualities and with calculating method gave the boy hell. The other assistants were treated with the compassion deserving nonentities. Shankland fed the fires of ambition in Jacklin by working him harder than the others, by giving him the dirty jobs and belittling his modest successes. He also taught him one of the soundest swings in modern golf.

Talking about those early days, Jacklin told me: 'Bill is one of my best friends today and there is nobody I admire more. But at the time I thought he was a bastard. I really hated him and there were times I could have killed him. Everything he did made me more determined to show him that I could do it; I wanted to win just so as to rub his nose in it. Looking back, I can see that it was all part of his plan and that he rode me because he really believed in me but it didn't seem like that at the time.'

82

Thanks to Shankland, Jacklin launched on to the world of competitive golf equipped with a consuming ambition and a swing which, when he learnt to control its tempo, could match shots with anyone. Inevitably he went to America after proving his ability with some notable British tournament victories and he immediately began to earn a respectable living. Then, in 1968, he whipped the best of the American players to win the Jacksonville Open to establish himself firmly as a great player. The following year he returned in triumph to win the Open Championship at Royal Lytham and St. Annes and in doing so not only confirmed his own stature but restored the fading prestige of British golf.

Jacklin is one of the most exciting—and therefore popular—of golfers in much the same style as Palmer. The brash confidence of youth is now usually sublimated into his game. Off the course he is the most modest and engaging of companions. But put him in a tight spot on the golf course and the aggression comes to the surface. I shall never forget one of his shots at the 1968 Masters when a wayward drive left him in the middle of a wood. Jacklin saw a gap no more than a yard wide and hit a full one-iron right up to the green. With the possible exception of Palmer, I know of no other player who would have attempted such a shot. Whether or not he will go on to win many more classic victories only time will tell. He has the game and the character for greatness.

A golfer remarked to Walter Hagen: 'You need luck to win an Open.' 'It may be luck to win it once' replied Hagen and on that discerning basis, the ability to repeat a classic victory, Jacklin's biggest test is yet to come. I think he will make it. I hope so.

5

Golf clubs and how not to throw them

BEFORE discussing the golf club we should first have a clear idea of the function it has to perform. In order to hit the ball far and straight and inherit the golfing kingdom four commandments must be obeyed: Thou shalt swing the clubhead fast; Thou shalt keep the face of the club square to the intended line of flight; Remember always to swing the clubhead along that line at the moment of impact; Thou shalt strike the ball at the correct angle of attack.

All bad shots stem from a breaking of one or more of these commandments. If the clubhead is moving slowly the shot is feeble; if the face contacts the ball at an angle sidespin is imparted to it and the result is a slice or hook; if the club approaches on the wrong line the ball is pushed out to the right or pulled left; and if the angle of attack is wrong the ball is either ballooned or scuffed along the ground. And that is really all that a player needs to know about the mechanics of golf.

Armed with those four facts he could, in theory, make a certain diagnosis of his faults by simple observation of how the ball behaved and then, still in theory, correct them. In practice it is not that easy.

An experienced instructor can diagnose other people's faults and suggest remedies but it is a rare golfer who sees himself objectively or, having done so, reacts rationally.

Take the common fault of slicing, where the ball starts straight but fades away to the right. Most of us who are afflicted by this complaint try to find a remedy among the recognized cures. We move the right hand over a bit, or concentrate on hitting through the ball, or close the stance. We experiment until we hit on the cause.

84

Our mistake is in thinking of the slice as the fault when really it is a side effect. Trying to cure a slice is like trying to cure a limp. There is no point in evening things up by walking with one foot in the gutter, or straining every muscle to stop the limp, or experimenting with novel techniques such as walking on tiptoe. And, of course, you do not do any of these things; you simply take the stone out of your shoe and the limp automatically stops.

That is an exaggerated example. It does, however, demonstrate the common trial-and-error approach of golfers to their problems. A rather more complicated golfing ailment proves the point. Say that you are hitting every shot with a low trajectory left of the target and with the ball tailing off left towards the end of its flight.

Faced with such an experience many golfers are too obsessed by their symptoms to analyse the causes. They concentrate all their thoughts on trying to keep the ball straight. But by referring to the four commandments it is obvious that the clubhead is approaching the ball from the wrong direction, on a line from out to in, and the face of the club is slightly turned inwards, or hooded, putting left-hand spin on the ball. Knowing the fault is halfway to curing it. Natural instincts are dangerous in golf because the swing is riddled by paradoxes—in order to get the ball high into the air you have to hit down on it; aiming left does not stop the ball bending away to the right, it makes the slice even more pronounced; for extra length, unless you are very skilled, you must swing more slowly. In trying to cure a fault the instinctive reaction is generally the wrong one. That is why the four commandments are so important. Everything in golf from the manufacture of clubs to the technique of the swing must be directed to them. They are the only absolute truths in the game. If they are observed then it does not matter if you grip the club with your hands the wrong way round, or stand on one leg or play with your eyes shut.

Teachers tell us, for instance, that a high finish with the weight balanced on the left foot is an 'essential' of a good swing. It isn't. It is merely the natural result of observing the commandments. If you could adequately fulfil those four conditions and yet finish flat on your back it would still be a good swing. One successful player, Chi Chi Rodriguez, occasionally does just that. If the four fundamentals are observed any unorthodoxy is permitted. A classic style is a beautiful, rhythmic movement of power and grace and is the most effective way of striking a golf ball because it conforms to the commandments. But the player who seeks style for its own sake is seeking a false god. Style is the result of a good swing, not the cause.

The teaching of golf is based on the accumulated wisdom of the past 500 years. The coming of high-speed photography compelled some small revisions—Harry Vardon believed that he played with a straight left arm, for instance, until the camera proved him mistaken—but the basic principles of the swing have been established with the authority of ancient writ. Teaching was based, and still is by many, on these traditional beliefs.

Then, with one blow from his slide-rule, a Welsh physicist sent half the edifice of golf lore tumbling into the dust. Dr. David Williams, a senior scientist at the Royal Aeronautical Establishment at Farnborough, where he worked, among other projects, on the design of the Concorde, the first supersonic jet airliner, was a golf addict. On his retirement he turned his attention to the technicailties of the game. He took an enlargement of a multiflash photograph of Bobby Jones's swing showing a superimposed sequence of 'frozen' images taken at intervals of $1/100$ sec. Since he knew the dimensions of the club and the weight of its component parts and could measure the amount of movement of club, hands and arms in each $1/100$ sec. interval, he was able to work out the exact force in operation during a perfect swing. The mathematics involved in Dr. Williams analysis are of a fairly elementary level, I gather, and his findings can be cross-checked by different methods. The forces which he demonstrated must be involved in swinging a golf club with maximum efficiency have been confirmed by measurement of instruments.

This is not the place and I am not the writer to go into the scientific details, but everyone can appreciate the main findings of his study. The first myth to be destroyed was the cherished theory

86

that big-hitting was the result of a powerful whip-lash action of the hands as the club head came into the 'hitting area' approaching the ball.

Dr. Williams showed that the hands, or more properly the wrists, contributed almost no power at impact. In fact, half the power came from the sweep of the club head past the line of the extended arms with the wrists acting virtually as free-bending hinges.

The swing is described by Dr. Williams as being in two parts. The first movement, starting from the top of the backswing position, is a 'fixed-body' rotation. That is, a turning movement around an axis through the neck and with arms, hands, clubs maintaining their relationship with each other. This is a slowly-accelerating movement and as the speed builds up centrifugal force acts on the club head and begins to pull it into a wider arc, with the wrists beginning to uncock. This starts the second phase of the swing with the power being supplied by a downward pull of the arms along the line of the shaft. The club head is thus drawn into its widest possible arc by increasing centrifugal force until at impact club and arms are in a straight line with the hands resisting a downward pull of nearly 100 lb.

All this is interesting enough to the serious student of the swing. For practical purposes it does not help too much. If the feeling during the swing is of a positive hit with the wrists at impact then clearly it does no harm to urge pupils to emulate this movement. Indeed, it may be necessary to *think* you are making a positive un-cocking movement of the wrists in order to achieve the desired, and opposite, effect.

But another of Dr. Williams's conclusions does have an ex-tremely practical application. Club makers have always maintained —indeed some still do—that extra power is supplied by a whipping action of the shaft snapping the club head into the ball. Dr. Williams proved this to be untrue and I will go into the details rather more fully when we come to consider clubs. More important, he showed that the degree of flexibility of a shaft did not affect the speed of the clubhead in any way. So another cherished myth bit the dust.

87

When I first wrote of Dr. Williams's findings that shaft flexibility contributed nothing to the power of a golf shot, I was inundated with letters accusing him of being a crank and me of being a gullible simpleton. What, I was asked, about the photographs actually showing the shaft bending forward as it strikes the ball. They were, said my correspondents, absolute proof of my madness. However, as well as all the photographs showing this phenomenon, there are others giving precisely the opposite effect: hands well *in front* of the ball at impact and with the shaft apparently bending backwards. And whenever this type of picture was reproduced in a book of instruction it was invariably accompanied by a caption pointing out that this was the prized 'late hit' of the master golfer.

Knowing as I did by then that arms and shaft form a straight line at impact, I reasoned that both types of picture could only be the result of an illusion arising from a trick of photography. I decided to mount an experiment which would convince the sceptics. In order to follow this experiment it is necessary to understand something of how a camera works. There are two types of camera shutter. With the compur (or iris) shutter, light is introduced to the sensitive film by a mechanism which operates like the blink of an eye. Starting with a pinprick the aperture widens to its full extent and snaps shut again. Every part of the film is exposed evenly and if there is a sudden movement by the subject it is represented on the resulting photograph as a blur. Hence racing cars have oval wheels. With an extremely fast movement the blur disappears to nothing and the golfer at impact is seen as holding an object which looks like a ghostly fan. The club head is not visible at all unless an extremely fast shutter speed is used.

The other standard type of shutter is the focal plane variety which is a roller blind with an open slit in it. In some cameras the blind travels from top to bottom, in others from bottom to top. And since photographers often hold their cameras sideways to get a landscape-shaped picture, it can be seen that the aperture slit in the moving blind can travel from top to bottom, bottom to top, left to right or right to left.

PLATE 1: *How the experiment was set up. Photographer Chris Smith devised a stand on which to mount five cameras, each with a different type of shutter action and all controlled by a single electrically-operated release-button. Before setting up the apparatus on the course the mechanism was tested in a laboratory to ensure that all the shutters were perfectly synchronized. Roger Fidler, the professional at West Kent Golf Club, took position and hit a drive which was thus recorded simultaneously by the five cameras at 1/500 sec. So all the pictures were of that precise moment of time (the variation in the level of the horizon is due to the fact that the cameras were on different levels).*

PLATE 4 (*opposite*): *This is the nearest representation to the truth. Another focal-plane shutter, this time moving laterally across the picture from left to right. (In fact it is almost exactly the same as the picture taken with the aperture moving in the opposite direction and, therefore, not reproduced.) Now the shaft looks almost straight, which is as it should be from this angle. It does bow at this point, but towards the camera. There is an enormous pull straight down the line of the shaft at this stage of the swing. If you stand on the toe of a club and pull the shaft you can reproduce the bowing effect of impact.*

PLATE 5 (*overleaf*): *Here is how the compur camera saw it, working on the principle of a blinking eye. The clubhead, moving at some 170 feet per second, is invisible and blurring is in proportion to the speed of all the different moving components. It is at this point in the swing that it used to be thought the hands 'poured in the power' and certainly that is the impression given by compur-shutter cameras just before impact. In fact, we now know that at this point the hands are exerting negligible sideways pressure on the club; the wrists are acting simply as hinges by this time.*

PLATE 2 (*above*): *On this camera the focal-plane aperture was moving from the bottom of the picture to the top. With this type of shutter the camera 'sees' the subject like the view of a station platform from the window of an express train. The first part of the scene it recorded was the clubhead. By the time its gaze had travelled upwards the upper part of the shaft had moved forward and the resulting impression is that the shaft is bending backwards at this point in the swing. 'The camera cannot lie' is a good public relations slogan for the photographic industry but its mendacity is proved on this occasion. This position represents the mythical 'late hit'.*

PLATE 3 (*right*): *This is the same moment in time. But on this camera the shutter was moving in the opposite direction, from top to bottom. As a result the hands were the first to be exposed on film and by the time the aperture had moved down to the bottom of the picture, the clubhead had moved on a considerable distance. The shaft seems to be bending forward into the shot and it is this type of picture which has given credence to the fallacious idea that the shaft snaps the clubhead forward at impact to give the ball an extra kick.*

We may ignore the complications of how the image which a camera 'sees' is turned upside down and reversed. For our purposes here we may assume the camera's view is the same as the human eye. So consider what happens with a focal plane camera whose aperture is moving from top to bottom. If the subject is a golfer at impact, his head is exposed first, then upper body, hands, club and legs and finally the club head and ball. But while the aperture is travelling downwards the club head is moving from left to right. And during the time it takes for the aperture to move down from hands to club head, that club head has advanced considerably. The effect, in the printed picture, is to show the club shaft as bending forwards. If the aperture is moving from top to bottom, we get the opposite effect and the shaft seems to be bending backwards.

The experiment I arranged with photographer Chris Smith was to mount five cameras on a stand and to synchronize them with a single electrically operated shutter release. The cameras were a compur and four focal planes, each with the aperture travelling in different directions. With this set up, he was able to take five pictures simultaneously. Each picture (between pages 88 and 89) is different although they all represent the same shot at precisely the same moment in time.

When the pictures were first published they excited some attention in the photographic world for it was thought that modern cameras were utterly accurate witnesses to the truth. These results reveal some important facts about the part played by the shaft of a golf club. It contributes nothing positive to the shot in the way of 'kicking into the ball', as had been universally supposed but in fact conforms to Bobby Jones's conception of it. He thought of the shaft as 'an imponderable connecting the club-head to the hands which can best be likened to a piece of string.' The rigidity in the shaft is of value only in preventing the club head from twisting.

One of the reasons why some experts were reluctant to accept these new ideas was the undoubted fact that elderly people and women *do* benefit from whippy shafts. However, the main reason for the improvement is not the extra flexibility but the fact that a whippy shaft is *lighter* since flexibility is governed by the thickness of the wall of the tubing.

A manufacturer told me a rather cynical little story which illustrates the way golfers delude themselves about shafts. A world-famous tournament player who plays with shafts so stiff that they have to be made to special order, broke one of his clubs and returned it to the factory for urgent repair. However, they had none of the special shafts in stock, so they fitted a normal 'medium' shaft and stuck on a label reading 'Ultra stiff shaft for . . . only'. The player is using that club to this day and has no idea of the deception.

Although manufacturers stress the precision of their products, shafts do vary quite considerably, as the experience of Billy Casper proves. For years he drove the ball with a slight fade. Early in 1968 he broke his driver and had a new shaft fitted. When he got the club back he found he was hitting the ball farther than ever before and, for the first time in his life, with a slight draw.

His swing, of course, was exactly the same. So how can the change be explained? Billy Casper did not try; he was delighted to accept the bounty without question. But an explanation must be possible.

Referring back to the golfers' commandments, we can deduce that Casper's fade was due to sidespin caused by the club face being fractionally open at impact. And since subsequent events proved that the golfer was not at fault this opening of the face can only have been induced by the shaft itself. The new shaft, although of similar flex, must have been more resistant to torsion, in some way, thus holding the club face 'closed' and putting draw on the ball. This would automatically produce a longer drive.

An advance in golf club design was signalled by the introduction of aluminium alloy shafts. They are lighter by half an ounce— a significant amount in the context of golf club dynamics—than their steel counterparts. And being slightly fatter in section they are more resistant to torque. Many club makers use this saving of weight to add extra weight to the heads. Their aim is to 'concentrate the weight where it counts, behind the ball'. In many advertisements for clubs we see the formula E (distance) = M (mass) × V (club head velocity). The clear implication is that, given the same swing speed, the heavier the club head the farther you will hit the ball. For the golfer this represents a misleading and dangerous half-truth. It ignores entirely the physical limitations of the player, not to mention other scientific complications.

The following example puts the position in perspective. Take a player who hits a drive 200 yards. If he adds 2 oz. to the weight of his driver and is able to swing it at the same speed (a highly doubtful assumption), he would drive the ball only an extra five yards. If he *reduced* the weight of his driver by 2 oz. he would lose five yards and hit the ball 195 yards. But if as a result of taking away these 2 oz. he was able to swing the club 20 per cent faster (a not unreasonable expectation for a lissom player) he would more than make up the difference, hitting the ball 215 yards. Weaker players, specially women, might well find they can hit the ball further with 'less powerful' clubs, that is with lighter clubs, not heavier. Aluminium shafts offer the opportunity of such clubs, but only if the headweight is kept the same or even slightly reduced.

Apart from this technical advantage, aluminium shafts help the golfer, specially the longer handicap players, by making him more conscious of the feel of the club head. For my own part, they give me a confidence that I can control the swing and bring the club head accurately into the ball. It is safe to predict that in the future as club makers become more aware of the scientific function of their products, they will concentrate research on discovering ever-lighter shafts. In this connection golf may well benefit from aero-space research which is ever exploring lighter and tougher materials. I can hardly wait to get my hands on a set of hydrocarbon-fibres.

The findings of Dr. Williams were confirmed and augmented by a group of scientists who were commissioned to study the swing by the Golf Society of Great Britain. Simultaneously, and working independently, technicians of the Dunlop Sports company were investigating the newly established principles of what happens during the swing and, more important, seeking ways of putting them into practical effect.

Although the introduction of steel shafts had been hailed as an important advance, in some ways it marked a decline in club-making techniques. Steel, being so much lighter and more twist-resistant than hickory, the clubs were a great improvement and the makers were lulled into complacency by the properties of the material. They concentrated their energies on techniques of mass production and marketing; and although they brought out new models each year it cannot be said that the newcomers were invariably improvements. They were different but not necessarily better.

The old craftsmen club maker working with hickory spent hours scraping at the shaft, pausing frequently for trial swings, until the club felt right. Then he did the same with another club until it 'matched' its fellow with a similar feel. With the arrival of steel, club making ceased to be a cottage industry and moved into the factory. The engineers took over and although they acknowledged the value of matching clubs they had no instruments to do the job which had been performed by the sensitive and experienced hands of their predecessors. The engineers had to find some method of measuring 'feel' and so the system of swing-weight was devised. The club is clamped in a machine at a point twelve inches from the top of the grip and a measurement is taken which relates the weight of the club to its length. Clubs vary in length by half an inch progressions and by adjustment in weight it is possible to produce a set whose swing-weights are identical. For years this was the standard method of matching clubs so that, in theory, they all felt the same to the golfer. As soon as they began to look at this system objectively the Dunlop scientists realized that it was based on several fallacies. For a start, a golfer does not hold his club twelve inches from the top of the grip and he does not hold it still. He swings it. And once an object such as a club is swung in pendulum fashion, a different set of natural laws becomes involved.

They determined that clubs must be matched in accordance with their behaviour during the swing. The moment of inertia—in lay terms the 'feel' of a swinging object—must be identical for every club in the set and they devised machines to measure these qualities.

In my belief they did not entirely succeed in solving this problem but the fact that they recognized the problem at all is a considerable advance. By itself, matching of clubs does not affect the shot, it contributes nothing to the impact of club head on ball. What it does, of course, is to influence the golfer. By giving him a uniformity of feeling he can swing every club with the same rhythm and therefore his consistency is improved. That is obvious enough but it is an important factor when we come to consider the shaft. As we have seen, the shaft does not of itself affect the shot in any way but it does affect the golfer. And it is here—the part played by the shaft—that more confusion arises than in any other aspect of golf technology.

The theory used to be that the shaft bent back at the top of the backswing and twanged forward at impact, putting extra zing into the shot. It is a beautiful idea but unfortunately the facts discredit it. Golf club shafts vibrate at the rate of about five oscillations per second and the downswing takes a third of a second. So the timing of a shaft's vibrations do not fit. Then there is truly high-speed photography, as distinct from the misleading pictures shown here. From photographs in which the action has been accurately frozen we can confirm the mathematical evidence that the shaft is straight well before impact and the club head, far from accelerating, is actually freewheeling at its maximum speed well before the ball is struck.

A third and rather simpler proof can be shown by observation. At the point in the swing when maximum force is being applied, and when the shaft could be presumed to be flexed backwards to the largest degree, the face of the club head is 'open' at right angles to the line of the shot. So when the club head is turned square to the line at impact, any whipping recoil of the shaft would be in quite the wrong direction and would simply put sidespin on the ball.

The significance of this conclusion is obvious. It destroyed all the mystique about shafts. We now know that all the major forces on the swing are applied longitudinally along the lines of the shaft and not laterally at all. The shaft's function, so far as transferring energy from the golfer to the ball was concerned, is simply to connect hands and club head and, subject to the need to prevent the club head from twisting, could be completely flexible.

This revelation took some of the magic out of the trick artist's performances. Paul Hahn uses drivers with jointed shafts and even a length of garden hose. Joe Kirkwood, who toured the world with Walter Hagen giving exhibitions of trick shots, hit the longest drives of his career with a club whose shaft was a flexible thong of rhinoceros hide.

So the flexibility does not help the shot and yet it was equally obvious from practical experience that different shafts did affect the player and the difference could not be entirely explained by the fact that whippy shafts are lighter. The actual flexibility came into it in some way. The Dunlop technicians devised a new type of shaft to fit in with their idea of matching the 'feel' of clubs during the swing. If shafts of standard flex are fitted to a set, the recovery rate of bending—or oscillation speed—varies from club to club because of differences in length and weight. They decided that what was needed, therefore, was to vary the degree of flex in every shaft in such a way that every club would vibrate at the same rate. To the golfer clubs fitted with these 'synchronized' shafts all feel the same and this may well help him 'time' his shots consistently with identical muscular responses.

The third improvement which the company introduced was made to act directly on the ball rather than on the player. In the conventional club, the hosel (or neck) of the head is fairly long and accounts for quite a large proportion of the weight of the head. The affect is to place the centre of gravity not in the middle of the club face, where it ought to be, but in towards the neck in the dangerous shanking area. What was thought to be the 'sweet spot' or 'power point' was neither sweet nor powerful. A ball hitting the centre of the face was actually half an inch from the centre of gravity and this gave the club a tendency to twist at impact and throw the shot off line. It also, incidentally, produced that glorious 'thwack' which has always been regarded as the proof of hitting the ball right on the button, and that equally satisfying shock wave up the shaft to the hands. It felt good and sounded good. In fact, if a ball is hit exactly at the centre of gravity, it sounds and feels to our conditioned senses, rather soft. Using these new clubs I was often surprised at the distances the ball went from what felt like a 'nothing' shot. What Dunlops did was to shorten the hosel and redistribute the saving in weight so the centre of gravity was really in the middle of the club face.

This was one change which could be analysed scientifically since it was a mechanical rather than a psychological improvement. A machine hit sixty balls with a conventional three-iron and then sixty with a three-iron incorporating the new principles. The difference in average length of the shots was not remarkable, about three yards, but the improvement in *consistency* was dramatic. Where the balls from the conventional club were spread over twenty yards, the new club hit them into a much tighter pattern of only half that variation. The improvement in performance in the hands of golfers were more marked, as would be expected since the major changes were calculated to react on human sensitivity and Dunlops decided to switch production of all their models to the new system of matching feel, sychronized shafts and balanced heads.

At the time of writing, this company is the pioneer in the field of scientific research—and there is much still to be done—but I am confident that their action is the beginning of a revolution in club design which will stimulate the entire industry. However the conventional club is far from dead or even seriously threatened. Goodness knows, the pros do well enough with it to inspire confidence and if the day is coming when clubs will be fundamentally different, that day is a long way ahead. The changes will surely be gradual.

In buying clubs the golfer must still exercise great care. The club which swings itself cannot be bought even though some over-enthusiastic advertisers might try to persuade us to the contrary. And no club will ever put more energy into the ball than the player puts into the club; the forces of Madison Avenue can never overcome the forces of nature.

Golfers believe themselves to be a bit more intelligent than the usual run of sportsmen. It is a harmless conceit and arises, I think, from the fact that the game has nothing about it of what Patric Dickinson, the poet golfer, has called 'the flannelled foolery and muddied oafery' of some other sports. In fact, a lifetime of golf has a beneficial effect on the character. It gives a man a philosophical attitude, tempers the temper and instils patience, restraint and good manners. It is a civilizing influence and of all the great players I have known I can count on the fingers of one hand the ones I would prefer not to have as neighbours. But wisdom, no.

As a breed golfers are simpletons. Once he gets to his golf club the most astute business man becomes easy meat for the huckster. A man who would never, even in the last excess of drink, buy a share priced half a point over the market valuation, becomes transformed as a golfer and clamours, figuratively speaking, for gold bricks and the deeds of Brooklyn Bridge. He buys a glove at double the usual price, because it is claimed to add '50, 75 . . . even 100 yards to your drive!' No exaggeration is too wild to arouse his critical instincts if there is the promise of an improvement in his game.

Friction-free tee pegs ('why lose unnecessary power?'), streamlined clubs to reduce wind resistance, special socks that put 'pow' into your leg-action . . . they all find a ready market. And no harm done, you may say.

But harm is done, seriously and frequently, in the biggest purchase of all which is, of course, the clubs themselves. Before the Second World War successful professionals were paid a royalty for every 'name' club they carried and this resulted in some pros taking thirty or more clubs with them, in bags so large and heavy that a man could hardly lift them. Legislation was passed to end this ludicrous practice by restricting golfers to a maximum of fourteen clubs. But this new law establishing a maximum had the incidental effect on golfers who had played happily all their lives with eight or nine clubs of making them feel deprived. Everyone wanted 'a full set' of fourteen clubs since the law had tacitly admitted that this number was necessary.

Manufacturers exploited the fourteen-club myth although, in fact, there is no such thing as a full set of clubs. Woods are normally sold in sets of four—driver, brassie, spoon and four wood. Irons are made from one to ten. And with a putter and a sand wedge the total comes to sixteen, so at least two clubs (normally the one iron and one of the woods) must be discarded.

Even so, the remaining fourteen are too many for most of us. Consider the evidence of the golfing machine which in the Dunlop's test produced a 'spread' of ten yards in hitting sixty balls with a three iron. A human golfer cannot hope to approach the consistency of a machine, even if he could judge distances to within a tolerance of five yards. (I doubt if one golfer in a hundred can measure a shot as close as that.) Yet iron clubs are graduated so that in the hands of a professional they increase in range by fifteen-yard intervals. A handicap player might hope to hit with two-thirds of the pro's power so that gives him a variation of ten yards per club. So even if he plays better than he knows how, hitting every shot perfectly, some of his four irons are going to go as far as some of his three irons. Clearly the handicap player needs fewer clubs spaced at wider intervals but he cannot get them. The best he can do is to buy a short set, say the odd numbers only. My experience is that if you throw out every other club the intervals are then just too wide; the jump from five to seven is too big. I have discussed this dilemma with many manufacturers and have not yet come across one who does not agree that a 'beginner's set' of irons spaced, say, at 3, 4½, 6, 7½, 9 would be sufficient. Yet the thought of customers being compelled to buy all nine irons is so appealing that not one of them, to my knowledge, produces such a set. The policy, I am sure, is short sighted.

Many other considerations should guide the prospective customer. It may be that Peter Thomson clubs are suitable for Peter Thomson. It does not follow that an identical set is perfect for you or me. That fact, so obvious, is ignored by 99 out of 100 customers. The normal method of buying clubs is for the golfer to approach his club professional. It would be nice to believe that all professionals are concerned only with the purchaser's interests. Not, alas, so. Pros are human, with normal business instincts. (There are honourable exceptions to this slanderous indictment but you have to search for them.) On being approached by a potential customer, the natural reflex is to bring out a set from stock and try a flattering sales pitch. And the customer, even more human and all too anxious to believe the flattery, waggles the clubs, is dazzled by the shining steel and brilliant plastic ferrules, and hauls out his cheque book. Such is the power of suggestion that his game will improve, at least temporarily.

Acquiring a new set of clubs is rather like getting married. The honeymoon is wonderful but how things go after that depends on whether the courtship has properly tested the true compatability of the partners. In some cases the affair settles down into a comfortable relationship with respect and genuine affection growing out of that initial passion. But all too often the bickering starts within weeks and life together goes sour.

I strongly recommend pre-marital golf to the swain contemplating taking unto himself a set of clubs. Consider the odds against finding a perfect match at first sight. A normal club can be supplied with a choice of at least three different types of grip, any combination of head-weight and shaft length, five grades of shaft flexibility and three angles of club head 'lie', flat, medium or upright. The possible permutations of these factors means that any single model can be made up in some 3,000 different combinations. Manufacturers are mass-producing clubs on averages. So the sets they distribute are medium everything: medium weight, medium length, medium lie, medium flexibility. Are you as medium as all that? Height, weight, physique, temperament, length of arms, occupation—all these can affect the type of club you ought to use. And the beauty of it is that it costs not a penny extra to buy a set of clubs tailored to your individual specification.

The makers don't exactly relish the idea of having all their customers order special sets since it is only by mass-production of their average clubs that they can keep their prices down. But they are all willing to make up special sets at no extra charge for the intelligent customer who knows what he wants and is willing to postpone his honeymoon for a few weeks in the interests of a lasting marriage.

Some club makers specialize in such orders and supply a detailed questionnaire on which prospective customers fill in their measurements. I would recommend going to an enlightened professional for guidance because he will be able to interpret the intangible factors. A man who is by nature slow and methodical will need heavier clubs, for instance, than someone of identical build but mercurial temperament: quick of thought and speech and briskly birdlike in action. Height alone is not the criterion for shaft length; the important measurement is the distance of the hands from the ground and the long-armed Neanderthal type whose knuckles are chapped from brushing over the dewy grass will be better off playing with short clubs even though he may stand seven feet tall.

Let us assume that you have worked out your specifications and know exactly what will suit you. There now comes the fun of choosing the brand, tempered according to how much we can afford to pay, of course. There is a wide choice of models available in the different price ranges and at last we can indulge our follies and vanities. Logic and commonsense can give way to instinct. To return to the wedding metaphor, we have been calculating and businesslike in telling the marriage bureau exactly what we want in size, shape and personality. Now we can begin to sort through the photographs and let our emotions take over. We can allow ourselves to be attracted. Rational thought has no part in this phase of falling in love.

Take this business of famous names. Most models have the autograph of a leading player engraved on the back. It is obvious that you don't hit the ball with the back of the club. It is, furthermore, equally obvious that golfers are not engineers or scientists and therefore, if they have any part at all in the design of the clubs, their contribution is the equivalent of inviting a great singer to assist in a tonsils operation. Never mind. Cannibals believe they derive the strength of their enemies by eating them, and the tradition of rugby

99

football was nourished in the Fiji Islands on a diet of Welsh missionaries. So if we are convinced that Jack Nicklaus's clubs will make us play like Jack Nicklaus, it will do us no harm at all to pander to our superstition.

The same applies to the pretty-coloured plastic insets, and to 'speed slots' and to the attraction of sculptured bumps and ridges, and to evocative words like dynamic, power-packed, super, shot-saver, and miracle-worker with which the golf-club industry woos the susceptible customer. They are cosmetics, useless but important. They make no basic difference to the product. But, as everyone knows—a lick of paint or a little strategic padding can work wonders for a woman—and the same is true for clubs.

Find a set that is fundamentally right for you. And then love it, cherish it, trust it and, above all, believe it to be the best in all the world. And golf happily ever after.

6

Trembling on the lip

PUTTING is half of golf. More accurately, perhaps, putting is an equal partner in the two games which comprise golf. They are two distinct activities. From tee to green a golfer is in the rational world. If he hits the ball straight it goes straight. And if it flies off line the explanation is to be found in the laws of dynamics. By and large he is rewarded according to his skill and punished in proportion for his mistakes. The hazards are there to be seen and avoided. The laws of cause and effect operate openly.

But once he gets on to the green he is through the looking-glass into a world where two and two don't always add up to four. It is a gambler's world where superstition is as important as logic and where intuition means almost as much as technique.

Non golfers find it rather bewildering. They see a man facing up to a three-foot putt which he has to hole for the Open Championship and they are baffled. It looks so simple. A flat, beautifully-prepared green, a hole of adequate proportions from that distance. 'Why is he dithering about like that? Why doesn't he just tap it in? I'm sure I could do it with one hand.'

And the non golfer could indeed do just that. An old lady could push it into the hole with the handle of her umbrella, a five-year-old could sink it with his beach spade. Anyone could hole it provided that it didn't matter. What makes it so difficult for the potential champion is that this putt is probably the most important action he will be called upon to perform in his entire life.

Take the analogy of an everyday action like eating. We all fork food into our mouths without stabbing ourselves in the face. We don't even think about it. But now imagine that a powerful electrical circuit has been arranged so that if the morsel on your fork happened to touch your lips you would be painfully electrocuted. That would change everything. An unconscious reflex action would now become significant. You would think about it, your hand would undoubtedly shake, you would watch the fork's journey very carefully. Suddenly the act of eating would become vitally important and consequently difficult.

All putts are important to a golfer and that's one of the things that makes putting difficult. And that is also why a non golfer can sometimes perform prodigies with a putter the first time he tries it, just because it does not matter.

There are other reasons why the Open champion suffers from that 'simple' three-footer. Greens look smooth but the path of a putt is seldom exactly straight. Irregularities in the texture of the putting-surface cause the ball to zig-zag, specially as its momentum falls. You can observe this by hitting a long putt on a flat green and then dropping to the ground and watching the ball from a worm's-eye-view. It oscillates noticeably. And sometimes, maddeningly, you can see this happening while you are standing over a putt; the ball veers off line just as it is heading straight for the hole.

This happens on even the most carefully manicured greens. But towards the end of a busy day greens become heavily worn. Henry Cotton worked out that 200 golfers impart 2,419,200 spike-marks from their shoes on the greens of a golf course during one day's play. Any one of those spike-marks could deflect a ball sufficiently to make it miss the hole from three feet. A deviation of three inches is quite common on a putt of twenty feet on a perfectly flat green. There are other difficulties for the putter. Grass is bent by the action of mowing-machines and a putt against the grain will require more force than one of similar length in the opposite direction.

In some parts of the world, notably South Africa, grass grows towards the direction of the rising sun and produces a distinct nap which deflects the path of a putt by as much as two feet in twenty feet of travel. Furthermore, few greens are exactly flat. On some courses, particularly at the seaside and in mountainous country, greens may appear to slope one way while in reality the fall is in the opposite direction.

Skill and experience enable a player to read the line of a putt. He can calculate how much to aim off to allow for slope and the nap of the grass but he can never determine how much the ball will be deflected by unseen irregularities in the surface.

Now I would not like to understate the part played by skill on the greens. A long putt which is correctly aimed is more likely to find the hole than a putt which is struck slightly off line. But it can happen that the bad putt will drop into the hole while the good putt misses. The fate of both is decided in some degree by chance.

The effect of all this on a golfer's nerves can be imagined. A man whose living depends on the game dare not allow the truth about luck to enter too largely into his thinking. From a distance of twenty feet, if a putt is struck on exactly the correct line, the chances of its dropping into the hole are no better than fifty-fifty. But the player who admitted that bleak statistic into his mind while addressing the putt could hardly avoid a measure of fatalism and consequently he could not muster his full attention to the making of the stroke. He would be at a disadvantage against the man who discounted luck entirely and, believing that skill alone was involved, concentrated all his faculties on the job.

Oscar Wilde's definition of faith as an unswerving belief in something you know to be untrue was never more true than in putting. You must believe that the fate of every putt is up to you and you alone, no matter how strong the evidence to the contrary. The true believer can thus be inspired to practice assiduously and approach every putt with a positive, determined attitude. And it pays off. For those twenty-footers he does at least get the true odds of even money where the waverers—or should we say the realists?—make themselves three-to-one against. Such self-deception is profitable. In tournament golf the saving of one stroke per round over a season, not an unreasonable return from shading the odds, can mean a difference in prize winnings of 100,000 dollars. Not a bad dividend from the fallacy of believing that if a putt is struck correctly it will go in every time.

Over the course of the years, however, the truth about the house percentage in putting is forced into the consciousness of the great players. Men who have earned substantial fortunes in prize money are often the most vulnerable. Having inherited the earth, the need for faith is perhaps no longer quite so strong in them. The accumulated experience of seeing ten thousand straight putts swerve away from the line rises up as a spectre of doubt which cannot be banished by incantation, bell, book or candle.

The truth is intolerable. And the effects are horrible, causing a form of paralysis known to golfers as the twitch, or yips. This malady has ended the careers of many a fine player. Just before he retired Ben Hogan was acknowledged by his fellow professionals to be, at fifty-five, still the finest striker of a golf ball among them all. But Hogan could not go on. The yips had him. During the American Open Championship of 1967 I saw this peerless golfer give a brilliant display of stroke-making but I could hardly bear to watch his agony on the greens.

The characteristic symptoms of a twitcher is a breakdown in communion between hands and brain. He knows what he has to do but cannot make his body respond. Having settled over the ball with club in hand, he finds himself unable to move. No matter how hard he tries he cannot bring the club head away from the ball. He is stuck, like Lot's wife, beaded with perspiration by the effort to break the deadlock. Eventually there is a convulsion as the player snaps the spell with a supreme effort of will but the action, or twitch, often bears little resemblance to what he intended. It is not uncommon for twitchers trying to hole a two-foot putt to send the ball scuttling twenty feet past the hole.

In its advanced stages, twitching is thought to be virtually incurable so far as tournament players are concerned. They have to retire from the competitive scene and although they may regain control on the greens for social golf the old trouble recurs as soon as they try to compete seriously again.

Among ordinary golfing mortals, and especially if the twitch is treated in its early stages, cures are common and in many cases the twitch merely runs its course like a common cold and vanishes in time of its own accord. For others a change of putter does the trick. Or putting one-handed, or simply changing the grip. Some sufferers obtain relief by the expedient of lining up the putt and then closing the eyes.

I have never been a good enough putter to run any danger of contracting the twitch but I have studied many victims and I believe that all but the most virulent cases can be helped. The aim must be to restore confidence and the first step in this direction is to discover some physical method of getting the club head smoothly into contact with the ball.

All putting methods depend on a movement of the arms or wrists, or a combination of both, and these are the areas affected by twitcher's paralysis. Fighting against it only makes matters worse so I advocate that the patient relies entirely on muscles which are still in good working order. In other words, he locks his hands, wrists and arms in complete immobility and moves the putter by swaying his entire frame from the hips, taking care to keep the head stationary as he does so. It is a most inferior method of putting but at least the player can retain a measure of control over his putts.

Naturally, if this is all he did, the twitch would quickly move downwards and would start to affect his legs. But if at the same time the seat of the trouble is tackled, that is in the mind, then the leg-putting technique will carry him through the period of treatment until a complete cure is effected.

The mental therapy must be directed at taking the tension out of putting by reducing its importance. Some suggest that the twitcher should divert his mind from the problem by doing mental arithmetic, reciting poetry (preferably not aloud) or thinking about sex. Again, I feel that this advice, although it may achieve temporary relief, does not get to the roots of the disorder. The fundamental cause of the twitch is over-anxiety combined with a complete breakdown in confidence. The only lasting cure can be obtained by changing the twitcher's outlook on putting. He must be made to realize that life will go on even if a three-footer is missed.

In a world of war, starvation and pestilence, a missed putt comes pretty low down in the scale of disasters but it is by no means easy to take the rational view when facing a putt. For the twitcher, locked in his private hell, the putt is the most important thing in the world for the simple reason that nothing else exists at that moment. A whiff of detachment, a realization by the twitcher that the putt is unimportant, that golf is unimportant and, above all, that he himself is unimportant, is all that is needed to blow away the fog in a golfer's brain and settle the nervous turmoil.

It is easier said than achieved. Golf is a game of carefully controlled balances. A good player must put himself under tension and yet be relaxed; he must steer a narrow course between confidence and complacency; he must be emotionally involved yet detached; concerned yet indifferent; fired up yet cool. When he meets disaster he must neither give way to anger nor suppress it; good luck must leave him without excessive elation but still inspire him; he must believe in himself totally while still retaining an image of the basic futility of what he is doing. On the practice ground there is not all that much to choose between the best players. What separates them in tournament play is the success they achieve in reconciling these delicate psychological equations.

To every successful golfer there comes a time when he is persuaded that what the world needs, above all, is a book. This is the Age of Communication. Every world crisis is presented as a problem of communication; neurotics complain that they cannot communicate. The communicators have taken over. They decree, through television, radio and the written word, how we shall live and what we shall think.

A telling case could be made that the progress of man is being stifled by over-communication. Faculties of freewill and enterprise which escape becoming atrophied from electronic bombardment are numbed by sheer weight of paper. You may well ask why, feeling as I do, I am adding my quota to the avalanche of words. A fair question. It is only a pathological vanity that persuades me that this book has the slightest virtue.

Certainly the world has no further need of books on how to play golf; there are far too many already. Some time ago I was asked to review a batch of new golf instruction books, about half a dozen since it was a slow month in the publishing world. The prospect was even less welcome than usual because I was technically on holiday at the time. I wrote that the only practical value of such works was to balance one on top of the head while practicing golf. When you can make a full swing without dislodging the book, I wrote testily, you will be a scratch player.

Later I rather regretted the ill-tempered tone of the review but I stand by the advice. A personal tutor with a gift for diagnosis and an understanding of the problems of each individual pupil is the way to learn and improve at golf. Books, no matter how sound, are too comprehensive. A learner can absorb and apply only about three points in a lesson. When he has mastered them and committed them to the realms of instinct then it is time enough to move on to the next stages. With a book the pupil gets it all in one indigestible lump and there are few sights on a golf course more ludicrous than a man who has just read an instructional chapter and is trying to remember and apply everything at once.

Paul Hahn, the American trick-shot artist, does an amusing parody of such a creature, reciting in a machine-gun delivery the essentials of the swing as he takes the club back and brings it into the ball for the inevitable fluff. A golf swing takes about one second to perform and that gives time for the player to concentrate no more than a single thought.

But if books are not needed this is far from saying that they are unwanted. There is a ready market for the thoughts of the latest Open Champion among handicap players who go through life under golf's Golden Delusion. This fantasy takes the form of a conviction that all they need to turn them into aces is one magic hint. Once this key is discovered everything will slip neatly into place, there will be a moment of revelation and they will take their places in the freemasonry of the scratch men. Instant Billy Caspers.

The legend of James Braid who became a long-driver literally overnight fosters the dream. But it's still a dream, I'm afraid, and nothing illustrates the cold awakening in golf books more clearly than chapters on putting.

Instruction on how to hold the club, how to stand and how to swing is fairly simple. Different players have small individual idiosyncrasies in their swings but essentially they are all trying to do the same thing and the basic requirements for hitting a golf ball are all too well known.

So most golf books rehash the same old facts and theories and fallacious ideas. The differences are mainly in emphasis. This player may stress the need for a straight left arm while that player will underline the role played by the right foot, but with a few outstanding exceptions golf books say the same things in different words.

Difficulties only arise when the famous man and his literary ghost have to tackle the subject of putting. There has to be a chapter on this important aspect of the game but what is there to be said about it? Some take the easy—and honest—way out by confining themselves to a description of their own methods. The unsatisfactory aspects of this approach is that nearly all golfers are exceedingly reluctant to claim that they are good putters. They seem to feel that a public admission of their superiority in this department would prove altogether too much of a temptation to the golfing fates who would exact instant retribution with an attack of the yips.

But, of course, no reader would want to copy the method of a player who rated himself an indifferent putter. So some authors suggest other players as models. This tactic is scarcely one to arouse the confidence of the reader either.

'The best putter I ever saw was Bobby Locke who used a rusty old blade putter and seemed to caress the ball into the hole with a gentle, sweeping motion. My own preference is for an aluminium mallet and I like to give the ball a short, sharp rap.' What do we make of that? We are shipwrecked and desperate for help and there is the captain telling us that we may jump for it or, on the other hand, we may equally well prefer to remain on board.

Our confidence has already been shaken by what might be termed the golf author's escape clause. This is really an announcement that what follows is valueless, and takes the form of a disclaimer along the following lines: 'Putting is such an individual matter that it is impossible to lay down dogmatic rules. Everyone must decide for himself what type of club to use, how best to hold it and what method he should employ in making the stroke. Only experience will tell you which is the most satisfactory combination for you. . . .'

At this point a sensible reader will move straight on to the next chapter, which is normally entitled 'The mental approach', but in the interests of research I have diligently read as much about putting as any man dare without endangering his sanity.

My purpose was to try and find any common denominators among the advice from good putters and thereby distil from the welter of confusion and contradiction a few drops of the essence of good putting. For nearly always there comes a point amid the waffle and the generalizations that the authors commit themselves to a direct statement. Raking over the heaped qualifications of 'some people find . . .' and 'In many cases . . .' and 'generally speaking . . .' these nuggets of unadorned, dogmatic conviction are there to be found.

'Take your putter straight back from the ball and straight through'—Ben Hogan. 'Swing it back slightly inside the target line'—John Jacobs.

'To produce solid, controlled putts you must constantly introduce the right amount of spin'—Jack Nicklaus. 'Any slight topspin, backspin or sidespin which can be applied to the ball by the putter will have no effect at all'—Golf Society of Great Britain's scientific research team.

'The head and body must be kept perfectly still'—Bill Cox. 'There should be no attempt to hold the body immovable'—Bobby Jones.

'Position the ball opposite the right foot'—Willie Park. 'Opposite the left foot'—Eric Brown. 'Centre'—Arnold Palmer.

'Strike the ball an upward blow with the club'—Tony Lema. 'Hit with a slightly descending blow'—Mickey Wright.

'Take the club head back low and in a direct line from the ball'— Bruce Devlin. 'For years I tried like fury to do both. Only in recent years have I appreciated that it is virtually impossible to do the first on any putt over about six feet and consistently make a square and solid strike; and that it is totally impossible to do both together and still make an easy, fluid and natural movement of the putter head'—John Jacobs.

They all agree, however, that it's a sound plan to keep the head still while putting.

But the conclusion is inescapable and depressing. To Gay Brewer's rash dictum 'There isn't a golfer born who can't become a good putter' we must add the rider 'But not from reading books'.

The fact is that the human body is ill-designed for putting in the manner required by the rules of golf. A frog, which can swivel its eyes independently, is better suited to the job. It could keep one eye on the hole and the other on the ball; we have to aim and then take our eyes off the target while we make the stroke. It is an unsatisfactory arrangement and many attempts have been made to rationalize the business of hitting a golf ball into the hole.

By far the most effective method was the shuffleboard push. Putters were devised with cylindrical heads and extremely long shafts; the player lined himself up behind the ball, facing straight at the hole, and with the head of the putter lying on the grass simply shoved it forward. It was blatently illegal and an outbreak of shuffleboard putting in Europe was promptly stamped out by the ruling authorities.

However, the advantages of having both eyes facing the hole while making a stroke had been demonstrated and further experiments resulted in the croquet putter. This, too, had a cylindrical head and a rather elongated shaft. The player stood astride the line of his putt and swung the club between his legs. Quite a croquet craze developed. Twitch sufferers took to croquet putting and a number of players who had abandoned golf returned happily to the game,

For a while we had quite a decent class of controversy about croquet putting. Like many others I thought it repugnant and felt it should be banned. If pressed to state our reasons we mainly stated that 'It just isn't golf'. Hardly an articulate and reasoned response, perhaps, but I still feel that it expressed the most valid argument against croquet putting. In fact, I also considered that Rule 19 covered the situation—'The ball shall be fairly struck at with the head of the club and must not be pushed, scraped or spooned'—but the wording is possibly ambiguous enough to admit of some argument.

Certainly the croquet brigade thought so. They put their case with fluent skill. It is, they said, perfectly legal, harmless and provides a method by which players who could not otherwise enjoy the game might continue to reap the benefits of golf. I don't know if anyone actually claimed that society would benefit from a re-claiming of fallen golfers by a reduction in the incidence of larceny, arson and rape, but the implication was there. Croquet putting could add in no small measure to the sum total of human happiness and fulfilment.

What is more, said the croquet putters in what they felt to be the clinching argument, what does it matter since no croquet putter has ever won any significant event. This was possibly the first time in history of man that there has been a powerful lobby for a change in the law on the grounds that the suggested reform was ineffectual. It smelled decidedly fishy.

Suspicions were justified by the evidence. Sam Snead was winning quite a lot of money in the United States using the new method and if he had won a major tournament, as he most assuredly would have done in time, the vogue for croquet putting must inevitably have reached epidemic proportions. The legislators of the Royal and Ancient Golf Club and the United States Golf Association met to consider the matter. In a last-ditch action, the croquet men raised the cry of 'Remember Walter Travis' in a desperate attempt to stem the rising tide of traditional outrage. The thrust, in my opinion, was aimed slightly below the belt.

Travis was the American golfer who won the British Amateur Championship at Sandwich in 1904. He was small and taciturn to the point of rudeness and he beat the pride of British golf with a display of putting which was quite uncanny. His putter was of a type which had never been seen before. It was called a Schenectady and, unlike all previous putters, the shaft went into the centre of the club head instead of being joined at the side of the blade. If Travis had been a warm, outgoing personality of the type most commonly found among golfing invaders from America things might have been different. But the manner of the man made the manner of his victory all the more unpalatable. And the R. and A., in what is generally accepted as a fit of pique, promptly banned centre-shafted putters.

They eventually removed the ban and their action in doing so was seen as a public apology to Travis and a withdrawal of the implication that his 1904 victory had been gained by unfair means. Whether the R. and A. did in fact feel any sense of contrition, I do not know, but when the name of Travis was brought into the croquet argument, no one was in any doubt how to interpret it; base motives were prompting the R. and A. again.

Happily the R. and A. and the U.S.G.A. were not to be deflected from what they saw as their duty. They banned croquet putting and, surprisingly, the subject died an instant death. I say that this was surprising because the new law simply decreed that in putting a player should not stand with one foot on or astride the line (or an extension of it) of the putt.

Now although this does in effect rule out croquet putting in its original form, it by no means prevents players from facing the hole when they putt. If anyone seriously believes in this method, all he has to do now is to play the ball from outside his right foot, instead of between the feet. He would retain all the advantages which were claimed with such vehemence for the original croquet style. The fact that the club itself can no longer have the shaft entering the head at right angle is no disadvantage; it helps to have it set at a slight angle.

Yet the only person I know who tried to persevere with a modified (and legal) form of croquet putting was Sam Snead with his side-winder method. For me, this above all proves the hollowness of the croquet-putting campaign.

If Snead's variation is too extreme then players can still adopt their old croquet method without infringing any law by the simple expedient of standing on one leg. No one, I think, has even tried that.

And so the only result of that entire unhappy incident is that we now have yet another rule on the books and it is one which is broken more often than any other. The convention of not standing on the line of an opponent's putt is a demonstration of good manners rather than of any practical value and it is meticulously observed. What frequently happens is that we leave ourselves a six-inch putt and in setting ourselves to tap it into the hole we straddle in a grotesque posture in order to avoid standing on the other man's line. But we forget, in extending this courtesy, that all too often we have put a foot astride an extension of the line of our own tiny, unconsidered putt. Someday this unthinking gesture of politeness is going to backfire; a player will be penalized just as he makes the ritual tap-in for a championship and what a fuss that will create.

What part does putting play in the modern game? This is a question which is asked increasingly and reflects a growing feeling that putting is disproportionately important.

In the early days of golf the holes were long even by today's standards. The original seven-hole course at Blackheath, near London, one of the earliest recorded clubs, had two holes of over 500 yards and the five holes at Leith, in Scotland, totalled 2,231 yards. With the equipment of those days a good player needed four shots to get up to the hole.

We do not know how large the hole was in those days; there does not seem to have been any accepted standard but judging by contemporary pictures they measured as much as six or eight inches across. And although prepared putting surfaces were not known (players were required to tee up within a yard of the hole) we can assume that two putts would be considered normal. No great premium was put on putting skill because of the nature of the ground surrounding the hole and putting can be said to account for no more than a third of the game at most.

With the development of prepared greens, putting has grown vastly in importance. For a par 72 course the first-class player is expected to go round in 36 putts and 36 other shots of all kinds.

But I believe that putting has come to dominate the game to an extent that is well beyond the mathematical fifty-fifty proportion and has made golf at the highest levels lopsided.

There is nothing new, of course, in the paradox that a one-inch putt counts the same as a 250-yard drive. That is part of the charm of the game.

What has changed the balance of the game is the preparation of courses. These days it is accepted among all but the most reactionary traditionalists that the more the element of chance can be taken out of the game the better. It should, we feel, be as much a game of skill as possible.

Modern design and course maintenance means by and large that from tee to green the golfer is rewarded or punished in proportion to his skill. He gets what he plays. On the green, however, he is at the mercy of fate.

The proof of this can be shown by experiment. The Golf Society of Great Britain used a machine which could be aimed with the accuracy of a rifle to discover an optimum level of putting performance. It missed 2 per cent of putts from 6 feet, 50 per cent from 20 feet and 80 per cent from 60 feet. Theoretically it should have holed everything and we must accept that the misses were due to the nature of the green itself. In other words, these figures represent an accurate measurement of the luck element.

Even so, the machine performed much better than any human golfer. The United States Golf Association keeps statistics of putting in the Open Championship and as a result we have a precise measure of how good a putter you have to be to win the Open. You must hole

everything up to 2½ feet, sink half of the 7-footers and hole out with
1 putt in every 7 tries from 20 feet.

These figures were corroborated by Golf Society experiments.
Their professional holes 55 per cent of 6-footers, sank 12 out of 100
putts from 20 feet (against 14 for the U.S. Open Champion) and
missed 97 times out of 100 from 60 feet.

The conclusion which I choose to draw from these figures is that
the luck factor plays too large a part in putting and that one way
to reduce it—and at the same time reduce the importance of putting
in the overall golfing scheme—would be to have a larger hole.

The Golf Society also tried some experiments with an 8½-inch
hole, twice the standard size. Fifty balls were played from different
distances with the following results: from 6 feet 44 balls were holed
and 6 missed; from 15 feet 20 were sunk in one putt, the remaining
30 needed a second putt; from 45 feet 9 balls were holed in one,
40 in two putts and 1 required a third putt; pitching from 50 yards
2 balls were holed out, 36 were down in two, and 12 in three.

The researchers reckoned that on this basis a scratch player would
save six shots in a round. They did not, however, accept that the
larger hole would necessarily reduce the importance of putting.
The bad putters, they said, would simply be twitching on six-footers
instead of three.

My interpretation is slightly different. A saving of six putts reduces the importance of putting in relation to the rest of the game.
And the fact that bad putters can miss the large hole means that a
good putter would still retain an advantage from his superior skill.

I do not believe that it would be necessary to go so far as the Golf
Society's eight and a half-inch hole. Much the same level of improvement would be provided by a six-inch hole. The very appearance of a larger hole would increase the golfer's confidence and,
therefore, his striking. And there would be the additional benefit
that a larger hole allows the ball to be struck more firmly, since the
ball would not hop so readily over the hole and the player would
not be so apprehensive about missing the one back.

With a larger hole golfers would be encouraged to become better putters, it would encourage more accurate approach work (since the rewards would be that much more certain) and it would restore the game to something nearer its original form.

The present four and a quarter-inch hole was standardized in the St. Andrews code of 1893, hardly any time ago in the history of golf. It does not have the respectability of true antiquity. An enlargement would therefore outrage no valuable traditions. And above all, a larger hole would make golf a much more enjoyable game.

7

Woman's place is in the what?

FOUR women were playing a friendly game at Effingham Golf Club and as they were putting out a man burst from the bushes beside the green. The uncouth manner of the stranger's approach was as nothing compared to his appearance for, apart from a bowler hat, he was entirely naked.

Although naturally taken aback at the interruption, which at the very least was a breach of golfing etiquette in disturbing players during the act of putting, one sterling spirit among the foursome was neither dumbstruck nor dumbfounded. 'Are you', she asked imperiously in the twinset-and-pearls accent of the Home Counties, 'a member?' Receiving no satisfactory reply, she promptly dispatched the intruder with a well-aimed blow to the bowler with her eight iron.

Reading of this incident I was intrigued by her choice of club. Presumably she laid aside the putter she must have had ready to hand at the time, made a rapid appraisal of the shot that was required and accordingly taken out her eight. Her selection opens up an interesting area of speculation; most authorities with whom I have discussed the problem insist that the wedge is the only club for such occasions.

But even more interesting, surely, is the wording of her question in that moment of crisis. Are you a member? It sounds so utterly irrelevant. But was it? I suspect that it sprang direct from her subconscious, a reflex response to four centuries of brainwashing. If that poor, deranged nude had replied 'Yes, madam, I am in fact the chairman of the greens committee' would the eight iron have been stayed, even momentarily, in its avenging arc? Speculation is idle, but the question at least suggests the possibility.

For the woman golfer in Britain, God's rarest blessing though she may be, is compelled to bow the knee to the lordly male of the species. She is still a second-class citizen, the victim of petty prejudice, masculine condescension and, at times, outright humiliation.

The beheading of Mary, Queen of Scots is the first recorded act of discrimination against a woman golfer. Tongues were set wagging when she was observed knocking a ball about shortly after the murder of her husband. Her political enemies made great play of her heartless behaviour and although there was rather more to her execution than the fact that she played golf, it set a useful precedent. Four hundred years later male opinion is still influenced by that summary tradition. 'What shall we do about the lady members? Oh, chop off their heads.' Not quite as extreme as that perhaps, since these days we like to think of ourselves as enlightened, but the basic mood persists.

Some clubs ban women entirely although their numbers are steadily dwindling. Oddly enough, this trend is reversed in America where new all-male clubs are being formed. No one would deny that members of a private club are entitled to conduct their affairs to please themselves. If they choose to be stag it is nobody's business but their own. Where the militant feminist has a right, a duty even, to stick an exploratory nose into the affairs of a private club is in the case of those which admit women under rules of membership which would induce apoplexy in the authors of the United Nations charter on human rights.

One club has a bench seat which must not be profaned by the impress of a female bottom; at some places women may play only at prescribed times and have to vanish, like Cinderella, on the stroke of the clock regardless of the state of their matches; other clubs put the public rooms off limits to women or banish them to separate and inferior quarters; a midland club relegates the ladies to a side door and another insists that they may never use a certain flight of steps. No vote, no voice in the club's affairs and even, on occasion, dictation by male committees on how they shall dress. It must be admitted that the destiny which shapes our ends does so in over-liberal degree in the case of some women golfers but the question of whether they should wear trousers is surely one for their own discretion.

I remember an occasion at a swanky English club which allowed women on the course until noon provided that on no account they entered the sacred portals of the clubhouse. In the car park I met two women who had been out playing when one of them was taken unwell. Her partner was saying: 'Perhaps if I knocked on a window one of the men would hand out a glass of water.'

Another incident, at the Royal and Ancient Golf Club of St. Andrews, perfectly illustrates the status of women in the golfing scheme of things. A violent rainstorm broke during a tournament and the women spectators, having nowhere else to go, huddled for what protection they could find from the full fury of the squalls under the lee of the granite clubhouse.

After some time the spirits of this bedraggled group were cheered by the sight of a club servant approaching like a lifeboat through the tempest. The women smelled salvation. At last, they thought, they have taken pity on us. Our plight has softened their hearts; they are going to invite us to take shelter, possibly in some snug haven where they house the empty beer crates and the dustbins. 'Ladies, I have a message from the members,' said the functionary with unctuous smile, 'Would you mind putting down your umbrellas as they are obscuring the view of the course from the smoking room windows.'

The faults are not all on one side. It must be admitted that there is a type of woman golfer, thankfully in a minority, who can make a thundering nuisance of herself. She takes up golf as 'something to do' when the children are off her hands, just the time when a woman's capacity for mischief is strongest. Some wretched assistant teaches her the rudiments of the game and she is away, without much knowledge and no great interest in acquiring more. I still shudder at the memory of playing behind two women on a frosty morning when temporary greens were being used. One of them overhit the temporary and her ball came to rest in the middle of the proper green. She played it where it lay—with a wedge.

Sometimes they can give offence in all innocence. The bellowing of an injured male does not carry much beyond the adjacent fairway but the squawk of feminine disappointment can transfix a player at the top of his backswing four holes away. It's all a matter of pitch, I suppose.

Sympathy for the underprivileged female is further diluted by their own attitude. How they do hug their chains even as they demand equality. What they really want is the best of both worlds; women's rights must not be bartered for women's privileges. Banishment from the golfer's bar is a small sacrifice in defence of this doctrine.

One of the side effects of segregation is that women who are continually reminded of their inferiority take this attitude on to the course and expect to play inferior golf. It is the most destructive thought in the game. Even those who enjoy equality in their clubs are affected, as golfers, by an awareness of their femininity—I am a member of the weaker sex, therefore I can never hope to play as well as a man.

A few women manage to liberate themselves from this psychological corset. Babe Zaharias, the American Olympic athlete, saw herself simply as a golfer. She hit the ball as far as most men professionals. Surprisingly it was her touch for the delicate shots around the green which betrayed her. If she could have matched the men in this department she would have collected many more of their scalps.

In more recent times the examples of Catherine Lacoste, the French champion, and the modern breed of American 'proettes' come to mind. Mlle. Lacoste lays into the ball without any sort of inhibition and many men pros would gladly swap their tee shots for hers. Dignity is the least concern of the American girls who have their own tournament circuit.

Paradoxically, there is nothing more graceful than a girl golfer swinging the club at full throttle; the ones who try to look elegant simply appear ineffectual and slightly ridiculous. Bobby Jones said that the best golf swing he ever saw belonged to Joyce Wethered (Lady Heathcoat-Amory) yet those who remember during her championship career tell us that she was the most graceful of her contemporaries.

Sheer strength is not nearly so important as the efficient application of modest power, as I have been mortified to discover in playing with low-handicap women. But there is one manifest difference in physique and some of the more buxom women players have to lean forward to sight the ball at all at the address. Mrs. Nancy Hitchcock, one of the few women teaching professionals in Britain, advises that on no account should the bosom be cupped between the arms. She insists that the arms should go over the top.

This anatomical train of thought leads me to the subject of the ideal shape for golf. A study of the great players yields few firm conclusions. No one physical type has produced a preponderance of champions. Exceptionally tall men have proved outstandingly skilful, specially with finessed half-shots, but for every good big 'un you can point to a good little 'un. Gary Player is short and yet even his detractors at their least charitable could not deny that for one year (1965) he was the best in the world. No giants of equivalent golfing stature immediately suggest themselves but there are plenty of men whose height and skill are well above the norm.

Very tall players—I speak from frustrated experience—are handicapped because of extra difficulties in keeping balanced and because their eyes are so far from the ball. Every act of manual precision, such as threading a needle or painting a picture, calls for an optimum length of focus. In hitting a golf ball the tall man has to stoop in order to get his eyes into range for accurate work. (There is an added complication in that even if the tall man can focus adequately from an upright stance he cannot obtain satisfactory clubs longer than the standard length. So he is forced to stoop on two accounts. How considerate it is of nature, incidentally, to endow us tall people with even temperaments, otherwise the aggravations of living in a world in which everything—cars, furniture, airline seats—is slightly out of scale would surely drive us frantic.)

Contrary to conventional teaching, strength of arm and hand is not the prime source of golf power. Recent medical research has confirmed that the large muscles of the body, in the back and legs, generate most of the energy for the swing. So overall dimensions are less important than proportion. The ideal, then, is average height, short strong legs and a long back, long arms (to increase the arc of the swing) and large hands (for club control).

Alert readers may have recognized in this specification the figure of Arnold Palmer. Actually, Palmer deviates from my theory of perfection in one particular. He is exceptionally wide-shouldered, which usually denotes power but erratic control in a golfer. Many fine players, in fact, are rather round-shouldered, or become so, and do not have the appearance of athletes at all. In this appearances deceive. In a series of comparative tests among all types of sportsmen, conducted by the Loughborough college of physical education, professional golfers headed the list for fitness.

In one respect women have a physical advantage over men. Being proportionately wider at the hip they naturally have a lower centre of gravity, a definite aid to balance during the golf swing. Jack Leach's description of a good steeplechaser—the head of a duchess and the behind of a cook—is no less valid for many good women golfers.

Modern golf is a game of power and any girl who has her sights set at championship level would be well advised to concentrate on exercises for strengthening the legs and back. (It is not by coincidence that Jack Nicklaus, one of the longest hitters in golf when the mood takes him, has to wear specially tailored slacks to accommodate the massive muscular development of his thighs.)

Whether a girl should be ruled by ambition to the point of fanaticism is another question altogether. With the passing years muscle turns to flab. Sporting fame often leaves the legacy of a pear-shaped figure, as the bloated forms of ex-boxers and weightlifters testify. Girl athletes are constantly urged in the sporting press to dedicate themselves body and soul to becoming world-beaters. Of course dedication is necessary. But often, it seems to me, girls are asked to sacrifice themselves on the altar of national esteem. I sometimes wonder if we are not asking them to pay too high a price for transient glories. The grotesque mutations, lumbering hermaphrodites from Russia who brought women's athletics into disrepute, showed the potential dangers.

With boys there is at least a small, but real, chance of a lucrative professional career as reward for zealous application. So far, the same opportunities do not exist for girls except in the case of a player who is so outstanding that she could hold her own among the American proettes. And she will be a rare bird indeed. For the overwhelming majority of girl golfers, the sport should be a part of life—an important part if you like—but not life itself.

As it is a girl who wants to reach international standard in golf must be prepared to make many sacrifices. There are no short cuts even for the most gifted. She will have to devote all her spare time to practice and training and, unless she is lucky enough to have the backing of wealthy parents, she will probably have to take a dead-end job in winter and deny herself all the luxuries which mean so much to girls at that age in order to save a nest egg for the tournament season.

Less obvious deprivations are also involved. Dinah Oxley, the English international, told me that she frequently wondered whether golf at her level was worth the sacrifices. She often envied friends of her own age when she saw them going out in the evenings to enjoy themselves. Her own daily routine, every morning after working in an office, was a session of hitting golf balls into a net on the lawn by the light from the dining-room window. The hardships were balanced by the compensations, specially the opportunities for world travel, but occasionally the scales wavered.

Then she added something which I found rather sad. 'What I miss most of all is social golf. I can never go out and play for enjoyment. Every shot I hit is important, it has to be.' That remark gives an insight into the top level of amateur golf which is not generally appreciated. The cost of golf is golf itself. For golf without fun is indeed a bleak prospect and contradicts the usual definition of an amateur as a person who plays purely for enjoyment.

It is only too obvious that some of the men professionals experience few moments of joy while they are playing. In some extreme cases every round is a form of torture by nervous tension; some players cannot keep food down during a tournament; others suffer from insomnia. The kinship between the pro and the top amateur is much closer than between the extremes of club players. The blurring of the distinction between pro and amateur has resulted in suggestions from time to time for 'open' golf. It is argued that golf should follow the example of tennis and create a new category of registered player for the hybrid creature who inhabits the no-man's-land between full professionalism and genuine recreational golf.

According to the advocates of such schemes, which have much to commend them, the way would be cleared for the payment of expenses to national, and perhaps county, players and possibly for cash prizes. In one way the ideals of amateur sport would be strengthened rather than compromised by giving players financial help; golfers who cannot afford to play the full calendar of events would be drawn into the game and the base of amateur golf would automatically become more democratic. It might also prevent the sad business of promising young players turning pro prematurely and having to apply for reinstatement when they find they cannot make a living at the game.

If open golf ever comes in Britain the main problem will be to determine where the line should be drawn between amateur and registered player. Possibly the best way would be to leave it to voluntary declaration, a simple renunciation of the right to compete as a 'pure' amateur.

There is, however, a point in golf where the tigers and the rabbits separate naturally, although it would not necessarily be the appropriate line of demarcation for registered players even if the game's parliamentary draughtsmen could express it in legal terms. The tiger is concerned by his bad shots; the rabbit accepts bad shots as normal and rejoices at the odd good ones. If you are in any doubt about which category you come in, just ask yourself which of your shots you would describe as 'exceptional'.

If the majority of us must count ourselves in the rabbit class we may take comfort from the bonus which goes with our high scores; I am sure we get more pleasure from the game.

We may envy the stars. But the golfer who has reached the summit can only stay there or decline. Either way, he is subject to pressures of success. The satisfaction of winning a golf tournament, like any other achievement, is a perishable joy which must be replaced quickly by a new ambition.

We who travel in hope are the lucky ones, with every hint of improvement an excuse for rejoicing. Although any golfer who says of his game 'I am content' is a liar, it is possible at the lower end of the golfing scale to sublimate ambition almost entirely. This is specially true of women golfers. Most of them can enjoy the game for itself without nagging dreams of cups and medals.

Henry Longhurst adapted the definition of knitting as an activity which gives women something to think about while they are talking and described golf as something for them to do while they talk. And why not? The ancilliaries of golf—the gossip, the companionship and the drink in the clubhouse afterwards—are as important as the business with club and ball. What's more, anyone seeking to justify the time they spend at the course can reflect smugly that golf, as well as being enjoyable, is undoubtedly healthy, a glorious exception to Dorothy Parker's dictum about all life's pleasures being immoral, illegal or fattening.

Golf has much to offer women. And the converse is surely true, if only men would allow them to make their full contribution. The time is not far off. And when women do achieve complete equality it will not be through agitation on their part or enlightenment on the part of the men. Their victory will be won by the one force which always prevails against prejudice and other matters of principle—economic power.

In Britain we have a tradition of cheap golf and the only way that this happy state can be preserved is by extending the activities of golf clubs.

It is, as I have said, a case of utilizing the plant. The country club has developed so successfully in America that I was interested when a committee member of a mid-western club asked me for suggestions on how they might spend some of their surplus income. Members of this club, like many others in America, are obliged to buy a certain amount of scrip which can only be spent in the club. This ensures that the facilities are fully used and foils the members who might be tempted just to play golf and never spend a ha'penny in the place. The women, not to mention children, are essential to the success of such systems.

I will end this chapter on a cautionary note: wives should beware of partnering their husbands in mixed foursome's competitions unless their marriages are firmly based. One story (true) to emphasize this advice. A golfing wife had acquired one of those superstitious habits which can so easily grip a golfer with a force as strong as black magic spells on a primitive mind. In her case it took the form of a belief that she could only hit a good drive if she teed up her ball right against the tee marker. For non golfers I should explain that the marker is usually a wooden ball on a spike, like a giant pearl tie-pin, or a heavy concrete block.

On this occasion the magic failed and the poor woman missed the ball altogether. The ball remained undisturbed, sitting up on its peg and waiting to be hit. The duty of hitting it, of course, now fell to her husband. And he was a left-hander—which meant that with the ball so closely under the lee of the marker there was absolutely no way he could hit it. The only course open to him was to have an air-shot himself, just make a token stroke at the empty air so that it would be the turn of his wife for another attempt.

The normal disciplines of good manners might just about preserve an uneasy peace among strangers in such circumstances. But between husband and wife! The possible consequences are too horrible to contemplate.

8

You're supposed to enjoy it

TOWARDS the end of the last century Horace Hutchinson, the great amateur golfer and even greater historian of the game, wrote of professionals that they were feckless, reckless creatures who worked only when reduced to it by extremity. In those days the pro was, for much of his time, a superior grade of caddie and his higher scale of wages (3s. 6d. a day) said Hutchinson, 'ought to buy you a human being bound body and soul to your interests. This is quite consistent with his passing the most candid, and even the rudest, remarks upon your game. You can hardly expect these hard, bitter gentry to appreciate the pain which they inflict on your cultured, sensitive cuticle, or the beneficial influence of a milder treatment. They have no nerves to speak of, and they do not see why you should.'

The hard, bitter gentry came in for another broadside from Hutchinson: 'Especially to be reprobated is the practice at some clubs of offering a "drink" to a professional at the close of a round. If you leave him to himself there is no danger of his damaging his health by drinking too little. No golf professional is recorded to have died of thirst. On the other hand, the lives of many have been shortened and degraded by thirst too often satiated. Some of the clubs of the North would be greatly more pleasant places if a fixed price were authoratively named for the recompense of professional caddies and players. There is a delightful uncertainty upon this point which more than the actual cost deters many from taking out a professional. The "dour" silence in which he accepts your fee when you give him enough, and the sense of self-contempt for the moral weakness which prompts you to give him too much, are equally annoying with his open dissatisfaction and probable profanity if you give him too little.'

'On the whole, the professional is not a bad fellow. He has little morality; but he has good, reckless spirits, a ready wit and humour which is only denied to the Scotch by those who do not know them, and he will show a zeal and loyalty in defending your performances behind your back—provided you over-pay him sufficiently—very much at variance with the opinion which he expresses to your face. He is apt to be insolent in order to show you that he imagines himself to have some self-respect—which is a self-delusion—but if you can endure a certain measure of this, he is a good companion. Never, however, bet with him; for so will it be best for him and best for you, as he is unlikely to pay you if he loses. This he is apt to do, for he is a bad judge of the merits of a golf match, a point which requires a delicacy of estimate normally beyond his powers.'

How has the picture of the professional changed in the eighty years since Hutchinson wrote that description? In the case of certain caddies, hardly at all. The ranks of travelling caddies who follow the tournament circuit still contain feckless, reckless, hard bitter gentry who run no risk at all of damaging their health by drinking too little and to whom the inside of a prison is a familiar, and sometimes welcome, haven during the off-season.

The club golf professional (as distinct from the professional golfer, or tournament player) has progressed a long way since Hutchinson's day. His emancipation was achieved by the example of two players of exactly opposed temperament. By the twenties the pro had evolved to the status of respected non-commissioned officer. He changed his boots in the caddie-master's hut, reported for duty on the first tee in uniform of Norfolk jacket, tweed cap and drainpipe bag of hickory clubs and deferentially 'sirred' the gentry. Walter Hagen, being an American, was insensitive to social distinctions. He naturally equated status with wealth and although he was not a millionaire he was the next best thing—he lived like one. By such actions as turning up on the tee in his dinner jacket after a late party and treating the Prince of Wales like a brother, his impact on the orderly stratification of golfing society was like the thrust of a walking-stick into an ant's nest.

Things could never be the same again. The feller couldn't be ignored; the quality of his golf, and of the man himself, ensured that he was accepted. It might have happened that Hagen would be treated as an exception, a unique creature and a foreigner at that for whom allowances must be made. Henry Cotton saw to it that this was not the case. Like Hagen, Cotton was not driven by any crusading zeal. He would never, I think, have described himself as a conscious social reformer. In his case, he looked at the rules of the caste game and decided that he did not want to play. Like many (or most) champions he was a loner. He stayed at the best hotels and arrived at tournaments already changed for golf, driving up in an impressive limousine. He was undoubtedly a professional and yet, equally obviously but in utter contradiction, a public-school man and a gentleman. He couldn't be ignored. He was invited in—and a precedent was established. The door was open for his fellow pros to follow which they did, slowly and sheepishly at first perhaps, but in increasing numbers and growing self-confidence. In 1968 Cotton achieved the ultimate emancipation when, with Bobby Locke and Hagen, he was invited to become an honorary member of the Royal and Ancient Golf Club of St. Andrews.

There are still some clubs where the pro is not allowed inside the clubhouse—or only at the express invitation of a member—but their number is dwindling steadily and the diehards are mainly run by men who are themselves unsure of their standing in the community. There is no snob like the man who has no justification for feeling himself superior.

On most of the charges brought by Horace Hutchinson the golf pro of today can plead not guilty. In one respect, however, he remains magnificently and indomitably second rate. Being essentially a solitary game, golf breeds an independence of spirit and

I

co-operation between pros, as the P.G.A.s have painfully experienced in Britain and America, is difficult to achieve, and complete harmony impossible. In a way it is admirable, much better
than the apathy which leaves control of some trade unions in the
hands of a minority of activists, for instance. Pros are all militant
activists in pursuit of their individual ideas. A common purpose
cannot be said to be their strength.

Although this attitude makes them more interesting as people it
puts them at the mercy of the golf industry. When it was announced that a top-grade golf ball was to be sold through a chain
of petrol stations at tenpence below the regular price, many pros
whimpered that the bread and butter was being snatched from their
hungry mouths. It is difficult to work up a sweat of indignation or
even sympathy for the pros in this type of predicament.

It is not necessary to be a captain of industry to see that the pros
have the power to prevent such incidents if they chose to mobilize
their strength. They control something like 2,000 shops in Britain,
each with a captive pool of customers which together comprise the
entire golfing market. If the pros' shops were organized as a joint
enterprise, they would together comprise by far the most powerful
retail outlet in the business. They would clearly be so powerful,
indeed, that they could dictate to manufacturers any conditions
they wished.

No club maker, for instance, would even begin to plan production of a new line without prior consultation with the all-powerful
chain of shops. On such troubled subjects as mail-ordering sales,
discount stores and other forms of 'unfair competition' the pros
could call the tune to which big business must dance.

As it is, the trading influence of the pros is no more than a series
of independent corner shops. They are little men and, as such, fair
game for exploitation. United, they could dominate the entire
industry. That they choose not to do so is their business; but they
can hardly expect sympathy when their attitude brings troubles on
themselves. There is a widespread feeling among golf professionals,
to judge by their public utterances, that the world owes them a

living and that club members have a moral obligation to buy all their golf equipment from the pro's shop. Both these fallacies are dangerous.

Most golfers in my experience would prefer to support their own pro but their duty, as customers, is to themselves and if this means buying clubs at a department store at a discount then that is what they will, and should, do. How much better it would be if there were no conflict; if inclination and commonsense both led to the pro's shop where the prices were better than anywhere else, the after-sales service was the best and where old clubs were taken in part exchange. That could so easily be the situation. Then those hard, bitter men could complete the transformation from the days of Hutchinson and become pliant and benign—and rich.

If my strictures of the golf pro in his capacity as a shopkeeper are harsh, it is not because of any lack of goodwill on my part; rather it is goodwill which prompts my criticism. Even under the present disorganized system, I adore pro's shops. I am an addicted browser and, I blush to confess, a sucker for a novelty whether it is the latest extravagance from America or a relic of the past. And pros are good value as shopkeepers. They are mostly good talkers and worthy protagonists in an argument about the technical merits of their merchandise. I always make a point of having a snoop around the shop when I visit a strange club and if I was restricted to one piece of advice to a golfing novice it would be 'Make friends with your pro.' There are very, very few with whom this would not be a rewarding relationship. On that score Hutchinson is entirely up to date: the golf pro still has good, reckless spirits, a ready wit and humour and a candour bordering on rudeness about your game. You may, however, bet with him these days for he will pay up—although he is a better judge of the merits of a match than heretofore and will almost certainly win no matter how many handicap strokes you can screw out of him. And he is still a good companion.

One of the most attractive aspects of golf—indeed, there are people who would claim it as the game's main strength—is the system of handicapping, by which the best player can meet the worst on equal terms. In theory the rabbit would have exactly the same chance of victory as the tiger and the game would go to the player who managed to produce a little extra, a slight improvement on his usual form. In practice it does not always work out exactly right although basically this is due to the flaws of human nature rather than defects of the system. But before looking at the grading of golfers in detail we must take a quick look at how golf courses are assessed. The one depends entirely on the other.

In Britain the grading of golf holes is done on a strictly mathematical basis. Up to 250 yards is a par three; 250–475 yards is par four; and above 475 yards is par five. Since the first-class player is expected to require two putts on every green all holes, then, are either one-shotters, two-shotters, or three-shotters. It is not an entirely satisfactory system since it is geared to the long-hitters. Not many golfers can hit the ball 250 yards in normal conditions and I believe it would be more realistic to set the standards at 220 yards for par three and 425 yards for par four. Admittedly this would bring the par four greens into drive and pitch range for the bashers, but the answer then would be, as I have indicated earlier, to tighten up their target areas. One beneficial effect of a revision along the lines I have suggested is that it would at least give the shorter hitters and handicap players a theoretical chance of getting on the green in regulation figures. (Many clubs recognize this need and use a second method of grading by which, for example, the longer par fours are rated as Bogey fives. The bogey system has always struck me as being an archaic and quite unnecessary complication, specially as the term is used in America to denote a score of one over par.)

The unsatisfactory nature of the present par system is reflected in the decision of the golfing authorities to introduce yet another course rating known as the Standard Scratch Score. The S.S.S. is based on the total length of a course and represents the score which a scratch player would be expected to return playing off the medal tees in summer conditions. Thus if the course measures over 7,000 yards the S.S.S. is 74 and if it is 5,000 yards long the S.S.S. is 63. Both these courses might be rated at par 70. An addition may be made to the S.S.S. for courses of exceptional difficulty and daily adjustments can also be made to cover changes in the weather conditions. The theory of S.S.S. is beautiful. It grades courses on the basis of difficulty and provides a common framework for the allocation of handicaps. In practice S.S.S. is next to useless and, in my experience, in almost total disrepute. In theory a player's handicap should always be applied in conjunction with the S.S.S. of his home club. If, for instance, a 5-handicap man who plays on a course of S.S.S. 74 meets a 24-handicapper from a S.S.S. 60 course, they ought to consult the 'Corresponding Handicap Table'. And if they are playing together on a course of S.S.S. 68, the 5-handicap man would have to play off 1 and the 24-handicap man would be required to play off 26.

I personally doubt if the system has ever been put to serious use by golfers since it was introduced in 1925 and I take further leave to doubt whether one golfer in a thousand (a) even pretends to understand how the system works, (b) knows the S.S.S. of his own course, (c) cares, (d) knows where to find the corresponding Handicap Table, let alone how to apply it, (e) would thank you for raising the subject.

Furthermore, there is an additional complication. Imagine two golfers of pedantic and mathematical natures who agreed to apply the system for a match on a neutral course. It could well happen that all their advance calculations would go for nothing when they arrived on the first tee and discovered that the secretary, holding a damp finger aloft, changed the S.S.S. as they waited to tee off. They would have to adjust their adjustments before striking a ball. To say that the S.S.S. system works is no defence against the hard reality of the situation which is that no one works it. That being the case, what can be done about handicaps? No subject in golf causes more bad feeling. Members are continuously resigning from clubs in protest at what they consider injustice at the hands of handicapping committees. To challenge a man's handicap is to impugn his honour and yet I doubt if one golfer in five plays off a handicap which truly represents his ability. On the Continent there is a widespread deceit among club golfers who like to represent themselves as being better players than they are. Visiting the continent I am constantly told that the British play to their handicaps and therefore have an advantage over the locals whose vanity forces them to masquerade under handicaps to which they have no chance of playing. And yet, when in Scotland and Ireland, I often hear complaints that English handicaps are pretentiously phoney.

If there is any injustice in this generalization—and we can all think of golfers who proudly cling to a single-figure rating when they cannot hope to break 90—then it is equally true that the Scots and Irish err in the opposite direction. In my own circle of Scottish friends I can count 24-handicap men to whom the handing over of the half-crown is a formality. It says much for their other qualities that I still count these rogues as friends. One such bandit went round a strange course in six over par and then had the gall to laugh as he trousered the money. My only consolation is the thought that in the normal way they have to play against each other.

But if the S.S.S. system is too complex what are we to use in its place? In America computers have been brought into the act and since it is the custom over there to complete a card every time you play, I daresay that the electronic mastermind can keep tabs on fluctuations of form very well. In Britain, however, we prefer match play and a good many golfers regard it as something of an imposition to have to submit cards. One solution which suggests itself to me is that club members should be required to play at least twice a year with the professional who would arbitrarily allot handicaps. The pros, I am sure, would welcome the opportunity (not to mention the income) of playing with all their members and they would automatically take course conditions and momentary aberrations into consideration.

And if I know club pros they could not be deceived by the occasional pot-hunting rascal trying deliberately to play below his

134

form. They are a pretty cute body of men in this respect. When I first met John Jacobs, the fine teacher of golf, we had lunch together and he asked me to describe the flight of the ball when I used a driver and a nine iron. On that evidence, plus a cursory glance at my grip on a fish knife, he guessed my handicap right to the stroke. Another advantage would be to bring professional and amateur golf closer together. To too many club members the pro is simply the man from whom they buy an occasional handful of tee pegs, a subject for violent complaint if he goes to play in a tournament ('What if I wanted a lesson?') and equally if he doesn't ('Why isn't he out there putting the club on the map?'). Both member and pro would benefit from closer association and the overall standard of British golf would undoubtedly rise as a result. A further desirable side effect of having the pro allot handicaps is that it would relieve the committee of a fair amount of the odium which is their natural lot. All they would be required to do is lend authority to the automatic reductions in the case of competition winners. When a man has the monthly medal in his hand it is awfully difficult to argue that his handicap should not go down. An absurdly proud smirk is the only reaction most of us can muster and one cause of friction in the bar would vanish.

So far I have not mentioned the rules of golf and although I recognize that a book which attempts to introduce the reader to a game must make at least a passing reference to its laws, I am reluctant to do so. The rules of golf consist of a lengthy schedule of definitions, forty-one major rules each with a number of sub-clauses, various appendices to cover special contingencies, and volumes of 'Decisions' by the Rules of Golf Committee to clarify obscure judicial points.

When I first became seriously involved with the game I was appalled at this complexity of regulations and, like others before me, tried to produce a simplified code, the bare iron rations of legislation for day to day consumption by club golfers. I was convinced that when playing in friendly matches for half-a-crown golfers would not need to concern themselves with the detail which might be necessary when great issues, such as the Open Championship, were at stake. Two factors caused me to change my opinion. In the first place whenever I attempted to set out a rule in brief, straightforward terms, I was inundated with letters on the lines: 'Your version of rule 35 is all very well so far as it goes but it does not cover the situation when . . .' And, of course, it didn't. To cover every situation you must have the official rule. Clearly golfers as a breed are rule-minded and enjoy arguing over knotty points of law. As a golf correspondent a large proportion of my post is from readers seeking a ruling on some obscurity or other. One, I recall, asked how many penalty strokes were involved in an incident in which a player left the flag in the hole while he putted and his ball, striking the flagstick, rebounded out of bounds! Freak occurrences like this happen all the time at golf and players, quite rightly, want to know the proper procedure. (The mistake they make is to write to me instead of to the Rules Committee.)

And so although I felt, and still do, that there was scope for simplification of some of the rules, I was discouraged from a personal crusade. The second factor which altered my view was experience of playing friendly golf. Like most people who play in regular 'schools' we got into the habit of adjusting some of the more oppressive rules in the cause of friendship. Not just giving putts, but playing preferred lies regardless of the time of year. That sort of thing. It sounds harmless enough, you may think, provided it was the same for everyone and indeed it was. But when I came to play in club and society competitions and had to obey the letter of the law, I found, not surprisingly, that scoring was much more difficult. Furthermore, a decent score was all the more satisfying for being strictly legal.

In one sense, golf is an easy game to cheat at. A nudge with the club head to improve the lie of the ball is undetectable and there are all sorts of dodges an unscrupulous player can pull. (While the majority of tournament stars are absolutely straight and regularly 'call' penalty shots on themselves when they alone could detect an infringement, there are a few notorious rule-benders about on the circuit.)

In another sense, however, cheating is impossible since in golf you are basically playing against yourself. The game is inside us and the challenge is to get it out. So if I improve the lie of my ball in the rough and hit it on to the green with a brassie I am robbing myself; there is no more satisfaction in it than turning the cards up one at a time in playing patience. I may 'beat' my opponent but the real victim is myself. On balance there is no satisfactory short cut through the rules. The best thing is to slog away at them and try to learn them thoroughly. It is, I admit, a forbidding prospect and I can offer only one positive suggestion to lighten the task. In Britain we have a tradition that it is bad form to use sporting rules to advantage: never question the umpire's decision, only cads and foreigners would stoop to such tactics as claiming victory by a study of the small print. There is no future for the golfer with a hang-up like that.

The rules of golf should not be seen as a list of prohibitions and penalties but as a Bill of Rights. If you are entitled to relief when, say, your ball drops into the grass-box of a mowing-machine on the green then there is absolutely no virtue in proclaiming that the spirit of the laws demand that the ball be played as it lies. Running alongside the machine hacking away among the grass clippings would display ignorance and stupidity rather than sportsmanship and, if I know green-keepers, a pungent comment to this effect would quickly be forthcoming. So learn the rules and then obey them meticulously—both when they penalize you and when they can be used to your advantage. I don't know how many championships have been lost because players did not know their rights; but I do know that Jack Nicklaus has won several tournaments because of his thorough knowledge of the laws. No player accepts a penalty more philosophically when it is deserved but if there is a loophole he knows it and, quite rightly, insists on the advantage. That seems to me to be an entirely proper attitude, far more admirable than ignorance and a stiff upper lip in adversity.

YOU'RE SUPPOSED TO ENJOY IT

People take up golf for a variety of reasons, all of them more or less harmless. Ambitious business types sometimes turn to golf as another professional skill, like doing a fast-reading course or computer studies, and very useful it can be too, now that so many deals are negotiated on the course and birdie talk has become the *lingua franca* of the commercial world.

Doctors frequently prescribe golf for patients who are running to fat in sedentary occupations although the medical profession is by no means unanimous on the value of once-a-week golf. At least one medical report has branded golf as a killer in certain conditions and certainly for people of uncontrollably volatile temperament it is, as they say, contra-indicated. Tournament players are prone to backache and a lifetime of intensive golf sometimes results in a rounding of the shoulders, a natural consequence of a crouching posture and as much an occupational disease as the elongated arm of a fast bowler. The main condition associated with golfers, however, is chronic hypochondria. Many of them play better when they are suffering from some slight ailment and if they don't have one they invent it. It is an interesting delusion, arising I suppose from the need to have a ready-made excuse to hand in case of failure, although there is a school of thought which holds that an ailment makes a golfer swing more slowly and therefore better. Or perhaps a nagging pain, real or imaginary, prevents the mind from wandering into distracting areas of speculation about the prize money or how they are swinging the club. Whatever the reason, the history of famous golfing victories reads like a medical dictionary—Ben Hogan, limping heavily from the car crash which nearly ended his golf career, as he won the U.S. Open in 1950; Ken Venturi in the last stages of exhaustion and supported by a doctor as he took the 1964 U.S. Open; Doug Sanders with his foot gashed open after stepping barefoot on a piece of broken glass and yet spreadeagling the field in the Peniscola Open in 1962.

Bruce Devlin won the biggest prize of his or anyone else's career by lifting the record Carling first prize of 35,000 dollars when he was convalescing from a varicose vein operation. Many players do not sleep, or eat, properly during big events but neither fatigue nor hunger prevents them from winning. There are many more examples of invalid supermen; Billy Casper, the most successful golfer of them all, suffers from allergies so obscure that at one time he had to live on a diet of rattlesnake and buffalo steaks.

The favourite standby is bursitis, a condition related to housemaid's knee. When all else fails, and a golfer is enjoying apparently perfect health, he can usually rely on a few psychosomatic twinges of bursitis to boost his confidence. Golf must be the only sport in which the discerning punter is encouraged by the sight of his selection receiving a pain-killing injection or bandaging an inflamed wrist. For most of us the pressures of golf will never bear heavily enough to force us into the esoteric realms of beneficial disabilities. We can enjoy the game and good health at the same time. And I suppose that the commonest reason for taking up golf is not to make a fortune or to clinch deals, but simply because of its intrinsic appeal.

It looks like a pleasant game, specially for those who have grown too old for more athletic sports. And it looks easy. The ball is not moving; it sits there waiting to be hit and you can take as much time as you like over the hitting. The novice takes club in hand, addresses the ball and takes a swing at it. Nine times out of ten he misses by about a foot. Now is the chance, if he wants to escape an obsession which may well transform his whole life, for him to say 'What a bloody silly way of spending your weekend', cast the club aside and dismiss the subject of golf from his mind for ever.

Human nature, however, is a ruthless slave-driver. The would-be golfer undergoes a bewildering sequence of emotions. Astonishment, embarrassment and frustration are submerged by determination. He tries again. And again. And again. By now the challenge is overpowering; he *must* hit that ball, his self-esteem is seriously threatened. It is absurd that a perfectly normal human being should be unable to hit a stationary ball which is fast turning into an enemy with an insolent sneer and hypnotic powers.

The novices' attitude, which started as faintly amused contempt and turned to blind anger, now changes again. He realizes that he is getting nowhere and if he is to keep his sanity he must approach the problem in a coldly rational manner. The ball is a doughty adversary, the trick is to match cunning with cunning. He takes the club back slowly, with as much care as approaching a sitting bluebottle with upraised fly-swot. The club descends, not very fast but with intense deliberation. There is a click, not unlike the sound which Hollywood would have us believe is made by John Wayne's clenched fist on a villain's jaw. The shock wave being absorbed by the shaft of the club is transmitted to the player as a sensuous tingle in the hands and forearms. And the ball, as it is picked up in flight by the wide-eyed gaze of the striker, is soaring straight and true into the far distance. At that moment a golfer is born. The memory of his first accidental good shot may have to sustain him through a tiresome period of learning. The pro makes him hold the club in a manner which is uncomfortable, unnatural and clearly ill-suited to the purpose. He hits a thousand shots that go scooting off along the ground to the left, or curl feebly into the right rough, or miss altogether with the head of the club burying itself into the ground behind the ball.

He learns the most complex set of rules known to sport, spends a small fortune on equipment and gives assurances about the religious persuasion of his ancestors in applying for membership of a club. All the while the memory of that one golden shot fortifies his ambition. And, in due course, there are other shots, raking drives, chips from 100 yards that run into the hole, miraculous recoveries from bush or bunker. There are plenty of bad ones as well but the glory of golf is that they are forgettable and forgotten.

It would be nice to be able to say of this type of novice that he takes up golf and lives happily ever after. Unfortunately, happiness is by no means automatic. Once a golfer is established in the game he should take stock of himself and decide exactly what it is about the game which he enjoys. There are several satisfactions from which to choose. The deepest joy is to improve and with sensible application and good instruction everyone can enjoy reducing his handicap. After a certain point, however, the graph of improvement which has been rising like a well-struck nine iron flattens out and the player must accept that unless he is prepared to devote an inordinate amount of time and energy to the game, his future progress will be considerably slower. We may live in hope that next time we shall find the secret: it is a harmless and indeed healthy delusion but most people have to work or raise families. Golf can claim only a small proportion of time; enough perhaps for a couple of games at weekends. If so, it is only sensible to take a rational view, spend the available time in playing for enjoyment and accepting improvements, if any, as extra bonuses.

In that case, with pleasure as the main aim, a distinction should be made. Some people like to wallop the ball. Fine. Let them wallop it. There are players who take four strokes at a short hole while their opponents take three but nevertheless enjoy the smug satisfaction of a moral victory at having got up with an eight iron while the lower-handicap opposition took a six iron. To such people three-putting is an irrelevance; length is all and golf is a trial of strength.

Another type of player gets his kicks from stylish golf. He is a perfectionist, more concerned with hitting good shots than effective ones. This attitude is normally a symptom of ambition, commonest among younger players who are working hard to improve. I must say I find it slightly tiresome when an opponent lays his ball stiff, three feet from the hole, with a full seven and slams his club down in anger because he hit the shot a bit thin.

But if scoring is what you enjoy then it is necessary to recognize the fact and adjust your attitude to this end. A correspondent, a retired engineer, who suffered a serious disability as the result of a car accident, wrote to me with details of his personal system which I consider is worthy of general application. He objectively assessed his own capacity with each club, on the modest basis of what he was confident of achieving rather than blue-moon exceptions. With this information he translated the card of his home course and set himself a new set of par figures.

As he put it, a beneficent committee had given him a number of handicap strokes to use as wisely as he could. The long par fours, the most difficult holes to score in regulation figures, he made par-fives. On such a hole he could just about reach the green if he hit his best drive followed by his best fairway wood. The odds against hitting two such wonder shots in succession were fantastic. However, by making the hole a par five he could take an easy four wood off the tee and then an easy five iron. That left him with seventy yards to cover in three more strokes, a push-over. And he only needed to hit one of those shots better than usual, pitching close or sinking a good putt, and he had a personal birdie.

The psychological advantage of picking up shots on par instead of dropping them was considerable. Obviously you cannot use this system of setting yourself a target and playing to a plan and at the same time indulge in heroics of enormous hitting. The two approaches are not compatible.

When I received this letter I indulged in an orgy of self-criticism and analysed my motives on the course. I decided that what I had been trying to do was not only to birdie every hole but with technically perfect strokes. No one in the history of the game has ever come within a mile of achieving that sort of standard. I felt thoroughly absurd at my own vainglorious fantasies. Since then, however, I like to think that my ambitions have been trimmed to something nearer my capabilities and certainly I have enjoyed my golf more.

And that, after all, is what golf is all about. It may be a banality but it is all too often forgotten. Golf should not be a battle in the lifemanship war, or a virility test, or a social asset or an excuse in gambling, or a character-building hobby, or an excuse for not taking the family out on Sundays, although it may contain elements of all of them. Essentially it is for amusement only. If it is played in that spirit it can be the most rewarding and satisfying game of them all and its fascination will endure for a lifetime.